TYTUS CZYŻEWSKI

A BURGLAR OF THE BETTER SORT
POEMS, DRAMATIC WORKS, THEORETICAL WRITINGS

A BURGLAR OF THE BETTER SORT
POEMS, DRAMATIC WORKS, THEORETICAL WRITINGS
by Tytus Czyżewski

Translated from the Polish and introduced by
Charles S. Kraszewski

This book has been published with the support
of the ©POLAND Translation Program

Publishers
Maxim Hodak & Max Mendor

Introduction © 2019, Charles S. Kraszewski

© 2019, Glagoslav Publications

Proofreading by Richard Coombes

www.glagoslav.com

ISBN: 978-1-912894-54-3
ISBN: 978-1-912894-55-0

First published in November 2019

A catalogue record for this book is available from the British Library.

This book is in copyright. No part of this publication may be reproduced, stored in a retrieval system or transmitted in any form or by any means without the prior permission in writing of the publisher, nor be otherwise circulated in any form of binding or cover other than that in which it is published without a similar condition, including this condition, being imposed on the subsequent purchaser.

TYTUS CZYŻEWSKI

A BURGLAR OF THE BETTER SORT
POEMS, DRAMATIC WORKS, THEORETICAL WRITINGS

Translated from the Polish
and introduced by Charles S. Kraszewski

GLAGOSLAV PUBLICATIONS

Contents

INTRODUCTION
TYTUS CZYŻEWSKI, SHAMAN 7

THE DEATH OF THE FAUN 48
THE GREEN EYE. FORMISTIC POEMS. ELECTRIC VISIONS . . 75
THE SNAKE, ORPHEUS AND EURYDICE 107
DONKEY AND SUN IN METAMORPHOSIS 115
A BURGLAR OF THE BETTER SORT 130
NIGHT – DAY 136
PASTORALS 176
ROBESPIERRE. RHAPSODY. CINEMA.
FROM ROMANTICISM TO CYNICISM 198
A LAJKONIK IN THE CLOUDS 226
SCATTERED POEMS 281
TEXTUAL NOTES 289
WORKS CITED 303

ABOUT THE AUTHOR 305
ABOUT THE TRANSLATOR 306

Tytus Czyżewski

1880 – 1945

Introduction

Tytus Czyżewski, Shaman

Benedetto Croce is quite right in reminding us that literary periods are of dubious value. To call Tytus Czyżewski a 'futurist' is to risk succumbing to an oversimplified approach to literary history that might begin with a point by point catalogue of *Parole in libertà* and proceed to work up a scorecard of Czyżewski's hits and misses. That's not how poets are formed. There is no handbook or instructions manual, and we should not expect Czyżewski to carefully thumb through the index of a well-worn copy of Marinetti's writings before deciding whether or not he's allowed to fit angels with prosthetic wings and send them buzzing about the skies over Poland in propeller-driven craft. A poet's compositional *ordo* is made up not only of whom they read — and the first major work of the present collection was composed a full two years before the *Manifesto de Futurismo* — but of who they are, where they live, and what they've experienced.

In the case of Czyżewski, even more important than literary movements that he consciously rejected (Romanticism, Symbolism) or aligned himself with (Futurism, Surrealism too — though perhaps less avidly) was the historical background of the nation of his birth.

In 1795, the already twice-partitioned, once mighty Polish-Lithuanian Commonwealth was completely wiped off the geopolitical map of Europe. More than a hundred years were to pass before its reestablishment at the conclusion of the First World War, and the breakup of the Empires of which it had once been part: Prussia, Russia, and Austro-Hungary. During the period of the Partitions, Poles were subjected to varying amounts of pressure — Russification and Germanisation. It is only logical that the main mission of the Polish artist during such times was the preservation of the Polish tongue, and Polish nationhood, amongst a population that was being encouraged, sometimes temptingly, sometimes harshly, to assimilate the national consciousness of a centralised government in Sankt Petersburg or

Berlin. As a result, Polish literature between the years 1795 and 1918 is patriotically and politically engaged. There is precious little of the autotelic among the writings of the Polish poets of the time in question. Very few Polish authors had the luxury of exclaiming, after Papini:

> In Italy, the Minister of Foreign Affairs is responsible for politics. Social matters are in the hands of the Minister of the Interior. I am concerned with literary affairs, and busy myself with them alone.[1]

Thus, when independence was re-established, it is not surprising to read, in the lines of even the more traditional poets of the first generation of 'free' Poles, such as Antoni Słonimski, sentiments like: 'My fatherland is free, free… / I shrug from my shoulders Konrad's cape'[2] or Jan Lechoń, whose words have become something of a slogan: 'And in the spring — let me see the spring, not Poland'.[3]

Perhaps because Czyżewski — who was nearly thirty when the map of Europe was redrawn by the victorious Entente — was born and raised in the ever more federalising, ever more liberal Austro-Hungarian Empire, where the individual languages and cultures of the ethnicities making it up were not nearly as oppressed as they were in Prussia or Russia, it is difficult to find the sort of xenophobic patriotism that animated the plebiscites set up by Woodrow Wilson and his collaborators at Versailles. It comes as no surprise to hear the parish priest in *The Death of the Faun* describe nineteenth century Poland in such terms:

> […] as for this country,
> It's gained a scar or two in roustabouts — —
> Unnecessary quite — but famous, ho!
> They're written up in histories, in fact.

---

1   Giovanni Papini, cited by Jerzy Kwiatkowski, *Dwudziestolecie międzywojenne* (Warsaw: PWN, 2012), p. 9. Unless otherwise noted, all translations into English are my own.

2   From his *Black Spring* [Czarna wiosna]; the reference is to Konrad, the hero of Adam Mickiewicz's *Forefathers' Eve* [Dziady].

3   From the *Magenta Poem* [Karmazynowy poemat]. Both of the citations come from Kwiatkowski, p. 11.

Czyżewski is perhaps being snide when, just previous to these lines, he has his priest apologetically explain to the classical creature:

> O, [...] we've a long way to go yet
> Until our nation's culture catches up
> With that of foreign parts

but, despite the offence that other Poles might take at hearing the armed uprisings of the Romantic age described as 'roustabouts', it's hard not to take the poet at his word when he calls them 'unnecessary quite'. For what, really, did they achieve? At any rate (although he is commenting on Czyżewski the painter, rather than the poet), it is worth underscoring the fact, along with Piotr Piotrowski,[4] that Czyżewski's engagement with contemporary currents in art predates the First World War. He does not merely arrive at 'purer' forms of artistic expression after 1918, when the obligation of 'organic work' no longer animated his pen. Now, I don't mean to say that Czyżewski was ambivalent to Poland or things Polish, but, rather, to point to him as an independent artistic force, who created on his own terms, letting his wider indigenous culture catch up with him at its own pace.

His poetic creations are basically apolitical. Czyżewski casts a sceptical eye on the conspiratorial traditions of the Romantics, whose time had passed away almost a full half-century by the time he was born, in lines like those that bring 'To the Manes of Juliusz Słowacki' to an end:

> In the netherworld, where those grey shades flit,
> Covered beneath the wings of gloomy night,
> Who yet of Lethe's waters have not sipped,
> Whose brows with misty musing still are bright,
> They hear, as they go into the death and dark,
> Echoing sevenfold, though it slowly thins,
> Like to a distant storm (though louder by far)
> Thunderous speech: 'The valorous deed, too, wins.'

The valorous deed wins… what, exactly? A place in national legend? Mention in what Mickiewicz calls the 'long nocturnal conversations

---

4   See Piotr Piotrowski, 'Od nacjonalizacji do socjalizacji polskiego modernizmu, 1913–1950', in *Artium quaestiones* 15 (2004): 97-138.

of one's countrymen?' They're still dead, Czyżewski notes, and as these belligerent, heroic shades proceed into the dark, it's not difficult to sense their bewilderment.

Rather than an ethnic, Polish patriotism, there is a very modern, European, feel to Czyżewski's sense of identity, which seems so like the twenty-first century idea of a 'Europe of regions,' but which really has its basis in the late Austro-Hungarian sense of commonwealth. There, loyalty was not focussed on any dangerous racial understanding of ontology, but rather on the person of the Emperor, the house of Habsburg. 'Other nations make war,' as the saying went, 'you, happy Austria, spread through marriage'. It is no surprise at all that in the many Christmas 'pastorals' that Czyżewski wrote, the setting is not a section of the Polish Tatras, but a natural cultural region that embraces both slopes of the mountains: Slovakia as well as Poland. The shepherds from Spiš have just as natural a place at the Child's crèche as their colleagues from the foothills around Zakopane. Not only the bandit Janosik feels at home on both sides of the border, which is nothing if not arbitrary.

TYTUS CZYŻEWSKI AND THE POLYMATH TRADITION

There is a long list of significant, multi-talented artists throughout Polish history. The twentieth century is particularly rich in individuals of great importance in more than one artistic field. Stanisław Wyspiański (1869–1907), one of the greatest Polish dramatists of all time,[5] is also the chief representative of Sezessionstil in Polish painting and decorative art. Stanisław Ignacy Witkiewicz ('Witkacy,' 1885–1939), made his mark as a writer of experimental novels, plays in 'pure' dramatic form, and an inimitable style of painting in which he made a careful study of the manner whereby self-administered narcotics affected his perception. Bruno Schulz (1892–1942), perhaps the most widely known Polish writer outside of Witold Gombrowicz, was a talented illustrator as well as the author of surrealistic cycles of narratives, which gained him the appellation of the Polish Kafka. Finally, there is Tadeusz Kantor (1915–1990) — avant-garde painter, theatrical revolutionary, who won worldwide recognition despite being shunned by the then-Communist

---

5   A volume of his plays centred in his native Kraków, *Acropolis: the Wawel Plays*, is available from Glagoslav.

government of his homeland, which looked upon his creativity with a less than benign eye.

Tytus Czyżewski, poet and painter, not only fits perfectly into this group, he is organically part of it. Witkiewicz and he trod the same paths as pioneers of Formism, before the latter set off on his own toward 'pure form;' Wyspiański was a professor at the Kraków Academy of Fine Arts at the time that Czyżewski studied there. Kantor, famous for declaring that '[for me it's] Wyspiański — in theatre, [Jacek] Malczewski in painting, and in literature — Bruno Schulz,'[6] whose first great theatrical triumphs came from idiosyncratic productions of Witkacy's plays, might well have added Czyżewski to that list. For he attended Czyżewski's lectures on art in Kraków,[7] resurrected, after the war, the Cricot theatre of which Czyżewski was part, with the aid of those who collaborated with Czyżewski in its original iteration — and perhaps even derived his penchant for mannequins and mechanised, almost ritualistic histrionics from the earlier poet's work in plays such as *A Burglar of the Better Sort*.

CZYŻEWSKI THE PAINTER

Czyżewski was born in the small southern town of Przyszowa, in the Tatra region, near the border with Slovakia. Between 1902 and 1907 he studied at the Kraków Academy of Fine Art. While there, he not only crossed paths with Wyspiański, who was on the faculty as professor of decorative arts, but sought him out:

> Wyspiański did not accept every student of the Academy to his atelier for the course on decorative painting. In order to be admitted, one had to prove to the master that one had a certain amount of talent, and knew quite a lot about painting in general. [… His fame was such that it] could only excite in my young mind the burning desire to belong to that unique school of his.[8]

---

6   Cited in Janusz Wałek, *Świat Wyspiańskiego* (Warsaw: Oficyna Wydawnicza "Nasza", 1994), p. 297.

7   Vide Krzysztof Pleśniarowicz, *Kantor* (Wrocław: Wydawnictwo Dolnośląskie, 1997), p. 31. The lectures took place in the Union of Plastic Artists [Związek plastyków] on the Plac Świętego Ducha in Kraków.

8   Tytus Czyżewski, 'Przy ul. Krowoderskiej' and 'Mistrz z ulicy Krowoderskiej,' first published in *ABC*, 27 November 1932, nr 345 pp. 110-113, and *Kurier polski* 1928,

Consequently, Czyżewski studied under Wyspiański from 1902–1903,[9] though he spent the lion's share of his time at the academy under the tutelage of two no less noteworthy Polish artists: Józef Mehoffer and Leon Wyczółkowski.[10] It is a testimony to Czyżewski's artistic genius that — like Wyspiański apprenticed to Jan Matejko — he was able to study under such strong artistic personalities, yet not fall into the trap of mannerism. Whether it was his five years in Paris (1907–1912), where he came to know the work of Cézanne and the Cubists, or his own irrepressible talent, he neither continued with the Art Nouveau of Wyspiański and Mehoffer, nor adopted the Symbolism, shading into an almost Bouguereau-like academicism, of Wyczółkowski, but pushed on to a very modern style of 'multiplane' compositions, 'uniting the the idea of the physical cube — the block — with simultaneity and fragmentary form'.[11]

Czyżewski's talent as a painter is such that, had he never written a line of poetry or drama, he would still be a noted figure in the European artistic firmament of the twentieth century. His fearless dedication to the creation of a new, contemporary art, especially his experiments in mixed media, point unerringly to the post-war work of Tadeusz Kantor. As fascinating as his work as a graphic artist is, however, we cannot allow ourselves the luxury of too wide an anabasis. Yet before we return to a consideration of his literary output, one more of his pronouncements on art is worth underlining. In the fourth issue of his journal *Formiści*, he wrote:

> The Polish nation must no longer subsist on the rotten remains of kings and forbears. The Polish nation must not become doped with the morphia of the nightmare of [Wyspiański's]

---

nr 13; cited here from Leon Płoszewski, ed, *Wyspiański w oczach współczesnych* (Kraków: Wydawnictwo Literackie, 1971), pp. 423, 420.

9   Płoszewski, p. 597.

10   Izabela Kunińska, ed. *Sztuka świata. Leksykon A-K*. (Warsaw: Arkady, 1998), p. 173.

11   Tadeusz Dobrowolski, *Malarstwo polskie ostatnich dwustu lat* (Wrocław: Ossolineum, 1989), p. 284.

Wedding [*Feast*], but it must feel in itself the art and poetry of the contemporary Renaissance.[12]

It is a splendid statement, in that it expresses his above-noted liberation, not only from the burden of national and patriotic engagement, but also from the slavish imitation of an artist whom, by his own admission, he practically worshipped. How similar this energetic slogan to Ezra Pound's nearly contemporaneous device, 'Make it new!' or, closer to home for Czyżewski, the concluding line of Apollinaire's 'La Victoire': *que tout ait un nom nouveau*.

INSPIRATION, AND THE POET AS PHOTOGRAPHIC PLATE

In the context of the Polish polymath tradition, how characteristic is the above quote of Czyżewski's, in which no distinction is made between painting and poetry as two modes of the same artistic expression that wells out of the artist, naturally. Of course, in considering the poetry of Czyżewski, the one formist element that leaps off the page is the manner in which he links the spoken word with the graphic image. For two brief examples of this, we may point to 'Hamlet in the Cellar,' a composite poem/graphic project from the volume *A Lajkonik in the Clouds* and, of course, the play *The Snake, Orpheus and Eurydice*. What are those figures interspersed between the lines of the former poem, that seem like the hieroglyphics etched onto golden plates and sent into the cosmos by the space agency, in an effort to provide sentient life with something to ponder when seeking to decipher anything of the civilisation that produced them? What, indeed, are the 'dynamopsychic stadia' that run down the right-hand margins of the latter play? It would be facile to call them mere illustrations. It is almost as if we — as non-artists — are some strange alien tribe to whom Czyżewski would dearly like to communicate something, some important message, but he doesn't quite know how. The keenest and most developed discussion of these images is given by Alicja Baluch in her article 'The Visual Nature of Tytus Czyżewski's Poetry,' of which we quote one brief passage:

---

12   Cited by Agnieszka Morawińska, *Polish Painting, 15th to 20th Century* (Warszawa: Auriga, 1984), p. 46. Translation by Bogna Piotrowska.

The most unconventional, and thus difficult to decipher, are drawings 1–12, which constitute the core of the action. Their various geometrical shapes present directional stresses, as an indication of the attraction and repulsion of masses (which was Witkacy's understanding of painting) — in this way one might interpret Czyżewski's drawings. Considering his own words, one might also acknowledge them to be 'dynamopsychic stadia, which occur at certain moments.' This is the description given in the introduction to the work. It permits one to suppose that there exists some language of the poet's own, hermetic and unapproachable by anyone else, in which he expresses underlying thoughts and emotions. They are the expression of inner experiences, as if they were sensory experiences, and therefore, they constitute the essence of symbolic language, through visual images. Erich Fromm states that we 'speak' this language when we dream, and the language of dream does not differ from the language of myth and religion.[13]

But if poetry is truly the art of speech and hearing, not of sight, how are we to deal with these images? The easy way out would be, along with Baluch, to suggest that the visual and verbal forms of *The Snake, Orpheus and Eurydice* are independent of one another.[14] That is easy, but not entirely satisfying. So, can *The Snake, Orpheus and Eurydice* be performed aloud? Can 'Hamlet in the Cellar?' Certainly. But we remain teased by the nagging suspicion that, without seeing the graphics, or experiencing them somehow otherwise in performance, we are missing out. The same thing can be said, surely, of the pictograms among Apollinaire's *Calligrammes*. Yet how different Czyżewski's interwoven images are from the word-pictures of that otherwise brilliant poet of the sublime *Alcools* — whom Czyżewski revered, and translated. Seen in comparison with these, Apollinaire's horses and cats and cellos made of poetic phrases seem rather exercises assigned by some particularly annoying elementary school teacher striving to awaken an artistic 'expressiveness' in her fidgety pupils. Czyżewski's dynamopsychic

---

13   Alicja Baluch, 'Wizualność poezji Tytusa Czyżewskiego' in *Rocznik naukowo-dydaktyczny* 101 (1986): 199-137, p. 130.
14   Baluch, pp. 129-130.

drawings, as mysterious and perhaps finally indecipherable as they may be, are yet something completely new in the completely new poetry he was pursuing — in 1922 and again in 1936 — and what is more, something important, authentic. Even if we don't quite know what to do with them in the performance of Czyżewski's poetic works, they are *real*. As Tadeusz Kantor might say, they are autonomous, even in the context of the works they accompany, perhaps, but still: they demand contemplation.[15]

It is somewhat curious that Czyżewski did not employ hieroglyphics (if that is the proper term) or ideograms, more often. The closest he comes to a synaesthetic approach in the purely verbal realm is in the poem 'Clairvoyant-Mechanical Photograph of the poet Bruno Jasieński.' The concept of this poem is astonishing in its simple novelty: it constitutes a comparison of the poem, to which the immediate image is so important, to the taking of a photograph. In its frank enthusiasm for the modern, mechanical form of portraiture which is photography, it makes a simple, yet eloquent statement about the objective, reproductive power of descriptive verse. Who is to say that the following surrealistic description:

> long hands are strolling about the room next door
> the brain is full of snakes and at this moment may be found
> in the kitchen on a frying pan
> grand amethyst eyes are swimming about
> along with the Christmas Eve carp in the bathtub
> long lunatic legs are descending from the sofa
> and creeping up on the commode
> fingers at this moment are playing on a clavichord
> 'god save the King'

is not as faithful a record of the inner reality of the poet-photographer's subject, as the chiaroscuro, mimicking depth and three dimensions, captured by the light-sensitive photographic plate? The creative

---

15 It is worth remarking here the influence that Czyżewski's art had on the development of Kantor's Independent Theatre [Teatr Niezależny]. See Pleśniarowicz, p. 64.

consciousness of the poet, like the mechanical apparatus of the camera, records what it is built to record.

This is where Czyżewski's spontaneity comes into play. It is not automatic writing that he pursues, like other futurists, but rather the state of being constantly open to impulses, which may jar him to the creation of art:

> 21 hours says
> my watch
> passing along the edges of the street
> I catch my foot
> against the door of a perruquier
> a new situation arises
> and thus a new direction in poetry
> 22 hours says
> my watch
> passing along the edges of the boulevard
> I catch my head
> against the leaves of a dry acacia
> from this nervo-situation
> a new direction in painting comes about

If Stendhal's ideal of the artist was a mirror walking down the street, that of Czyżewski is a walking, sensitive photographic plate. His spontaneity is the reception of impulses, which he then works into final shape through his process of poetic creation, which, as we have seen, is devoted to form (and thus not spontaneous). Curiously, Czyżewski seems here quite akin to Wordsworth, in the latter's confession to the creation of poetry as the 'spontaneous overflow of powerful feelings [...] recollected in tranquillity.'

THE SHAMANISTIC IMPULSE

Agnieszka Morawińska states that 'the painter and poet Tytus Czyżewski believed in the instinct of artistic creation, and in the act of creation being similar to birth in nature.'[16] Very true. This outpouring of creative energy, in visual or verbal form, is what he means when he swears his

---

16   Morawińska, p. 45.

allegiance to 'the instinctual art of the animals' in his programmatic brochure 'From the Machine to Animals:' '***The mechanistic instinct*** == *"let each one write, sculpt and paint **as** his **instinct** directs him!"'* Instinct here is to be understood as openness, the willingness to be directed to creativity by nature, the world around one, as if one were a shaman and the world — his (no coincidence!) 'animal master'. Although the creation of art is not to be a spontaneous matter — 'Just please,' he cries in the same text, 'no programmatic primitivities!' — nor is art a modish dalliance for the effete. 'Let us kill the "aestheticism" within us!' he proclaims, immediately following the former statement. It is as if he saw primitivity and aestheticism as antipodean opposites, both of which he rejects. Rather, he wishes to tap into something that he senses as the natural or creative artistic impulse of the universe:

> **Long live the electrical instinct**
> **the instinctual art of the animals**
> **the instinct electrical**
> of the cosmos
> of minerals plants beasts men
> of the inner life of the **medium.**

The artist should respond — naturally and unaffectedly — to this impulse as the plant does, in turning its leaves to the sunlight. If he were looking for a traditional religious trope, Czyżewski might have described this impulse as did his contemporary, the short-lived metaphysical poet Jerzy Liebert, as participation in God's original Creation. His younger contemporary and colleague, the Warsaw futurist poet Aleksander Wat, makes use of the taboo term 'primitive' in relation to Czyżewski's art, but in a way that emphasises his primal nature as an artist, tapping into the creative juices of the cosmos:

> Now Czyżewski was a phenomenon unto himself [*zjawisko bardzo odosobnione*]. The same thing can be said of his paintings — his Madonnas, the first formist Madonnas. I remember the first time I was in the Academy gallery in Venice, how struck I was by the similarity of Czyżewski's somewhat cubist Mother of God to an anonymous icon from the Italian primitives of the XIV century. In both poetry and painting Czyżewski had a lot in common

with *le Douanier* Rousseau. Now, this wasn't primitivism in the same sense as ours, but it was actually art from the very roots, from those primitives. He was, sort of, not so much a prophet as a shaman. His proximity to futurism and to novelty was caused by his shamanism, insofar as his visions and his words did not fit into logical, normal phrases. He was an authentic poet-shaman of great magnetic power.[17]

And so, as far as Czyżewski is concerned, the relationship of the true artist to the world, from which he naturally derives his artistic expression, is not that of a botanist or zoologist cataloguing the life that surrounds him, but rather that of a shaman who is able to penetrate to the creative depths that cause that life, in its variegated forms, to be. In speaking of shamanism, Joseph Campbell, building on Mircea Eliade, defines the shamanic experience as:

> a normal event for the gifted mind [...] when struck by and absorbing the force of what for lack of a better term we may call a hierophantic realisation: the realisation of 'something far more deeply interfused,' inhabiting both the round earth and one's own interior, which gives to the world a sacred character; an intuition of depth, absolutely inaccessible to the 'tough minded' honest hunters (whether it be dollars, guanaco pelts, or working hypotheses they are after), but which may present itself spontaneously to such as William James has named the 'tender minded' of our species. [...] The crisis [*of shamanic vision*] cannot be analysed as a rupture with society and the world. It is, on the contrary, an overpowering realisation of their depth.[18]

Czyżewski speaks of the artist's relationship to nature in a strikingly similar manner. He gives the clearest idea of his understanding of the artist and nature in the short programmatic essay 'From the Concept of Nature — to Nature Itself' included in *A Lajkonik in the Clouds*:

---

17   Aleksander Wat, *Mój wiek* (Warsaw: Czytelnik, 1991), vol. I, p. 52.
18   Joseph Campbell, *Primitive Mythology* (London: Penguin, 1985), pp. 252-253.

Nature is a constant mass (a body) — touched by the hands of a blind man. Touching things, the artist forms his own spatial world, upon which 'CONCEPT' of his depends his very entry into the AREA of nature. That nature has the same effect on him as a lightning storm has on a pagan. Wishing to create for himself (HIS OWN) concept of a storm, he must turn to art. […] Through abstract form — the artist approaches nature — since he must return — in order to discover his own spatial world — in order to be in the midst of that lightning storm — and not just view it, observe it, from the outside.

So, identification with nature? — NO!

To create one's own world from nature — not an abstract world, but ONE'S OWN.

A sculpture, a building, a painting, a poem — this is not an identification with nature, it is NOT THE ABSTRACTION OF SIGHT — it is nature, unconditionally itself. Materially and spatially individual. HARMONICALLY DEPENDENT upon the centre[19] of the lightning storm (nature) in which the human being (the artist) finds himself.

[…]

Disinterestedness plays no role — in art — nothing plays any role in art which is not me MYSELF — who creates an IMAGE or a poem, WHICH IS NATURE ITSELF, not identically but in the centre of the lightning storm.

Like the shaman, the artist separates himself from the everyday world and enters into the creative matrix of nature, from which he derives the message he brings — and all art is communication, after all — to the receptors, to us, who have no such ability to contact the very beating heart of things.[20] Again, Mircea Eliade:

---

19   *Ośrodek* — centre, hub, environment.

20   Thus I would somewhat differ with Leon Chwistek's defence of Czyżewski's individualism: 'Like every true artist, Czyżewski is completely sincere. He paints a bandit as he imagines him to be, in other words, he paints him as he comes across him in reality. And that's what it's all about, that Czyżewski's reality is something completely different from that, with which average people have to deal. Perhaps it is not beautiful, maybe it's even horrid, but it's different.' Of course, here Chwistek is picking up the gauntlet cast by Czyżewski's critics. While it is

The lands which the shaman sees and the personages whom he meets in the course of his ecstatic journeys into the beyond are meticulously described by the shaman himself, during or after the trance. The unknown and terrifying world of death takes form: it organises itself in conformity with specific types; it takes final shape as a structure; and, with time, it becomes familiar and acceptable.[21]

Now, just like the words of an ancient oracle, the message he brings carries more within itself than do the merely practical modes of our daily communication. Art is separated from all other forms of human expression by the form in which it is transmitted, and that form is also — perhaps even *primarily* — deeply eloquent and multivalent. Along these lines, the poem 'Return' alludes to some of the gigantic claims of Mickiewicz's shaman-poet Konrad in his Great Improvisation, but in a novel manner. Whereas the romantic bard is *above* nature, ruling it like a god, Czyżewski's narrator draws his strength *from* the springs of nature. He does not lord it over the birds, he needs them to aid his flight; he does not overtop nature, he loves it like a woman, and wishes to *return* to it (hence the title), to learn from 'granddad Gorilla.'

CZYŻEWSKI AND ANARCHICISED POETIC FORM.
THE INAPPLICABLE THEORY

Care with form as the main ingredient of art, form as content, form as the medium of expression that distinguishes works of art — especially poetic expression — from all other forms of human communication, is implied in the very name 'Formism.' It is a vital characteristic of Czyżewski's poetry. His verse, his theatrical works, are carefully crafted. They have nothing to do with automatic writing, or the Ginsbergian 'first

---

important to remember that context, it is equally important to stress that, however individual his expression, the artist is still attempting sincere communication with his receptor. I quote Chwistek from Stefan Konstańczak, 'Od Formizmu do Strefizmu. Ewolucja poglądów estetycznych Leona Chwistka,' in *Słupskie studia filozoficzne*,8 (2009): 13-29, p. 19.

21 Mircea Eliade, *A History of Religious Ideas. Vol. 3: From Muhammed to the Age of Reforms* (Chicago: University of Chicago Press, 1988), p. 20. Translation: Alf Hiltebeitel and Diane Apostolos-Cappadona.

thought — best thought' approach to poetry, which was to become ever more popular as the twentieth century drew on. As he writes in 'From Romanticism to Cynicism,'

> Through my constructions of poetic form I wish to rescue poetry from the jaws of death. For poetry, unfortunately, in recent times, and at the hands of people with no vocation thereto, has become piece-work 'more convenable to shoemakers than Apollo.' I endow each word that appears in my poetry with individual significance and autonomy; at the same time, via the anarchisation (not anarchy) of words, I separate them into groups of analogous words, from which I elicit analogous phrases, etc. For this reason, words and phrases, despite a frequently superficial alogicality, as a whole (through the contrast of bonding materials) result in a cohesive entity, which lives like an organism in the natural world.

This is dense prose — and not necessarily enlightening. His description of 'anarchisation' is especially challenging. We will try to define it better below. For now though, it is important to stress the importance of the poetic craft, that is, conscious dedication to poetic form, in Czyżewski's output. In the poem 'For Art and Life' from *The Green Eye*, he explicitly advises:

> *For the construction of worlds start*
> *With FORM*
> *[…]*
> *From art through STYLE to what abides*
> *The spirit to harmony inclines*
> *Where senseless form will have no part*
> *Where now is birthing the new art.*

The primacy of 'instinct' that he champions isn't reactive or mindless in creation, but rather an instinct to the proper harmonies of art — an instinctive attuning to the creative act. And so it is no coincidence that this poem, so unusual in its surrealistic images, is still expressed in the tight form of more or less regular couplets:

> *The day re-azures as dawn breaks*
> *A wave of spiral tremblings quake*

> *The atoms' nervous jerky throes*
> *The steep planetary roads*
> *Crackling radioactive currents*
> *Misty fires that sputter and dance*

Among the poems collected in this earliest volume of his verse, 'The Sleep of Flowers' and 'Rain,' certainly, and 'Cathedral' for all extents and purposes, are sonnets. 'Music from a Window' is composed in a form as intricate as any sestina or triolet.

Other poetic forms utilised by Czyżewski throughout his career, which saw the publication or production of nine major collections and plays[22] are significantly more inventive and idiosyncratic. Before we proceed to describe them, however, we should now touch upon the key matter of the 'anarchisation' of the word, which supposedly lies at the heart of his poetics. I say 'supposedly,' because whereas his poetry is fabulous, and his theory quite interesting — still never the twain shall meet. It is so difficult to square Czyżewski's theoretical pronouncements with his actual poetry, that it almost seems as if they were written by different authors, one knowing nothing of the other.

In the other programmatic essay included in *A Lajkonik in the Clouds*, 'On the Delogicalising of Poetry,' Czyżewski writes:

> The first, main task of contemporary poetry and prose is the elimination of the word from its enslavement to the logics of phrase and syntax. This has nothing to do with the symbolism of the word, i.e. with the bestowal upon the word of some planted, or artificial, or even tectonically accepted meaning. The word in poetry or in prose possesses a realistic meaning, which is autonomous in relation to other words set next to it, or even eventually linked to it, by the logical interpretation of thought.
> [...]
> According to the old poetical conception, 'horse' is also a synonym for running, war, a noble and sublime elevation — and

---

[22] A volume of poetry called *Antidotum*, which would have been his last collection of verse, was lost during the destruction that followed upon the Warsaw Uprising of 1944. The spiteful act of planned municipal destruction by the Nazis resulted in over half of the city being completely wiped off the map.

this idea reaches as far as symbolism and the symbolic conception of the word 'horse.' Should we add an attribute (an adjective) to this word, for example 'winged' = winged horse, we see how logically, idea-logically, and even symbolically, the word horse has been transformed, somewhat — even strengthened imagistically, conventionally, in a poetic sense.

It seems that Czyżewski is after a purification of the word from its historical and cultural accretions. This is not as hard to do as it seems at first glance. If the reader or critic, used to seeking allusions and working up interpretations from them, is warned *not* to, i.e. 'in this poem, *horse* means simply *horse*. Your interpretation will be invalid if you infuse that word with anything else but its simple meaning, as this was not the poet's intent,' the poet has at least a fighting chance to see an honest, bare-bones critical approach to his poem, which would treat the words as they are found, without delving 'beneath' them in search of allusions which, he insists, are not there. As a matter of fact, such an approach to the poem would refreshingly centre *it*, and not the critic's ingenuity, in the consciousness of the reader. So far, so good. He continues:

> [Marinetti and Apollinaire] began to use the word, I reckon, automatically, unthinkingly even, only for its innate value as such, what I call its 'autonomous' value. […] The word, in and of itself, cleansed of pseudo-values (which after all do not describe its sonoric-linguistic meaning) — automatically possesses value only in itself, and becomes the foundation of a new poetry, a new prose.

These terms echo those of his colleague, Anatol Stern, writing in the *Almanach Nowej Sztuki* [Almanach of the New Art] in 1924:

> The new art does not beautify reality — it transforms it. It has effected the autonomisation of aesthetics as an artistic method of constructing the world. In our thoroughgoing social expansion we based ourselves upon the non-mechanised instincts of human nature.[23]

---

23 Stern, p. 23.

The transformation of the reality, instinctual art — these are terms very similar to those of Czyżewski, quoted above. But how are we to understand 'autonomisation' — a term frequently on the lips of avant-garde poets of the period, from the Ultraists with their demand of the 'autonomy of the lyrical reality'[24] to Czyżewski's own 'anarchisation' of the poetic phrase?

Here is where the practical problems begin. 'Absolute' music exists side by side with programme music; the great twentieth-century painters and sculptors created 'absolute' varieties of their own arts via the rejection of representational, mimetic painting and sculpting, concentrating solely on the interplay of volume, line, mass and colour, without any reference to any object existing in the natural world. It is no wonder that the avant-garde poets were so well aware of trends in contemporary painting, nor is it a wonder that some of them, like Czyżewski, were painters themselves. But can there be an 'absolute' poetry? The poet can stand at the side of the reader, like a tense schoolmaster, ready to rap his knuckles should he expand the simple word 'horse' into allusive and allegorical meanings. But poems are not made up of one word, and when words are strung together, they cannot be appreciated without the use of logic, and that means, without the concretisation of the text by the reader. And that, inevitably, involves historical accretions of meaning.

Problems with absolute poetry occur when the poet proceeds from the autonomy of the word *eo ipso* to the autonomy of the word even in relation to the other words that surround it in a phrase. This is because human languages work, naturally, in such a way that the given word, no matter how autonomous, simply cannot help having its meanings altered by the context in which it is found. Words act upon one another in communicative phrases; words lose their autonomy, or at least a significant portion of it, when linked with other words in a phrase intended to communicate sensibly. It is one thing to tell a critic or a reader, 'When you come across "winged horse," see *winged horse* and nothing else. Any interpretation that finds in my winged horse an identification with Pegasus, or an allusion to poetry, is invalid.' But it becomes something quite different, inevitably, when the horse, winged or not, is put in close proximity with other words. 'Rust food horse' as a hypothetical poetic phrase might be approached as Czyżewski wants it

---

24 Stern, p. 19.

to be: rust is rust, food is food, and so on. But if a verb and a preposition are added to the phrase — as they almost invariably are in Czyżewski's own poetic practice, e.g. 'Rust is food for the horse', the autonomous meanings of each of these nouns has been diminished: rust is modified by its identification with food, and the horse is modified by his eating habits.

I do not mean to suggest that I see something here that Czyżewski does not, any more than I would dare pontificate on the meaning of his dynamopsychic stadia. But it is fair, I think, to stress that Czyżewski's theory outpaces his poetic practice. As such, however interesting his theoretical writings are, as theory, his poetry can be — indeed *must* be — appreciated without applying those theories to it.

When we return to the idea of 'absolute' painting, with which Czyżewski was familiar, it becomes apparent that although such autonomy theory is quite fitting in relation to the visual image, its applicability to literature is negligible. This is because of the nature of the material he must, perforce, use in his verbal creations: pre-existing language. It is this which must be abandoned, if an absolute poetry is to be created, as Isidore Isou comes close to doing in 'Larmes de jeune fille,' a poem that is nothing but form:

> M dngoun, m diahl Qana îou
> hsn îoun înhlianhl M pna iou
> vgaîn set i ouf! saî iaf
> fln plt i clouf! mglaî vaf
> L o là îhî cnn vîi
> snoubidi î pnn mîi
> A gohà îhîhî gnn gî
> klnbidi D blîglîhlî
> H mami chou a sprl
> scami Bgou cla ctrl
> gue! el înhî nî K grîn
> Klhogbidi S vî bîncî crîn
> cncn ff vsch gln iééé...
> gué rgn ss ouch clen dééé...
> chaîg gna pca hi
> Q snca grd kr di.[25]

---

25   Collected in George Steiner, *After Babel. Aspects of Language and Translation*

Only in this way can Apollinaire's desire, expressed in the programmatic 'La Victoire,' be achieved:

> Ô bouches l'homme est à la recherche d'un nouveau langage
> Auquel le grammairien d'aucune langue n'aura rien à dire
>
> [O mouths, man is searching for a new language
> Where there will be no place for the grammarian].

Yet here we must stop. That sort of poetry would be the death of poetry. This is not a matter of the destruction of quotidian logic in poetic expression, which allows for Czyżewski's singing bears and speaking wolves, angels whizzing about in aircraft, but of the destruction of *all* logic, which would cut our sight off completely from those marvellous, illogical poetic creations.[26]

For a poem like Isou's truly is a *poème clos,* as its subtitle proclaims. There is no entry into it — except for the title, which seems to suggest something like 'this is what a young girl's tears sound like.' Indeed, even the form here is autonomous. We see couplets, and even internal rhymes. But how can we be sure that we are pronouncing the poem correctly, when there is no referent outside it to aid us to its pronunciation, written, as it is, in no actual language, built up out of symbols that *look like* the Latin alphabet, but needn't be (or even if they are, needn't be pronounced as an Englishman, Pole, or Frenchman might pronounce them), and symbols that *look like* Greek (or Cyrillic) letters, but needn't be... Even

---

(Oxford: Oxford University Press, 1981), pp. 195-196. Steiner comments, among others: 'No signals, or very few apart from the title, are allowed to emerge and evoke a familiar tonal context. [...] The wall is at the same time blank and expressive'.

26   Writing in the introduction to the 1920 edition of *The Green Eye* (and thus, one would imagine, with the poet's approbation), Leon Chwistek further muddies the waters by suggesting that poetry 'is constrained to battle against the habit of the direct apprehension of the phrase with the almost complete neglect of form, and it can do so only through the avoidance of phrases linked to a relatively strictly defined content. This is why the great poets always sought out, more or less consciously, a certain adumbration of the content, so as to allow themselves to cast the brighter light upon the full charms of the language in which they were working (Dante, Słowacki).' Tytus Czyżewski, *Zielone oko. Poezje formistyczne. Elektryczne wizje* (Kraków: Gebethner i spółka, 1920), p.5.

the punctuation marks may not be punctuation marks, but symbols descriptive of sounds. Czyżewski never pushes so far in his anarchisation of speech. And this is why the following statements are so difficult to understand, so difficult to square with his actual poetic practice:

> If we take, for example, a certain number of words and by means of so called **anarchisation** link them together, providing them with autonomous, suggestive meaning, giving them in their gathering (the phrase) a lesser, or greater, logical or imaginative significance, we bring them closer to **the essential meaning of the word, as poetry.**
>
> [...]
>
> The complete break with what had been up till now the 'logicality' of poetry, under whatever term it was known: Romanticism or Symbolism, leads to the creation of **suggestive poetry**, the poetry of **true realism.**
>
> The word, as a sound, or as a suggestion, as the essential voice of nature: the song of birds, the voices of animals, the songs of aboriginal peoples — is the foundation of the poetic autonomy of the word, which leads to completely new, broad possibilities in prose and poetry.

How do Czyżewski's 'suggestions' differ from the built-in allusions that words accrete over the years, and against which he struggles? Even *Robespierre*, which he references in this essay as an example of the above, doesn't provide us with the most convincing evidence. Unless it be that in his careful, but not fully developed, distinction between 'anarchisation' and 'anarchy' he means that 'anarchisation' does not negate a sensible flow of ideas, whereas 'anarchy' (as above, exemplified by Isou) would, it is hard to see what he is getting at by insisting upon the forbidding of allegorical reading, the 'complete break with the logicality of poetry.' For as splendidly surrealistic as *Robespierre* is, it still tells a logical (*sic*) story of the French tyrant of liberty faced with his ultimate failure.

In a way, ironically, the failure of Robespierre to establish new norms, norms independent of the moral order of the world established by the God he would arrest and abolish, is coterminous with Czyżewski's own inability to turn established human speech into a new course, independent of its millennia of development.

TYTUS CZYŻEWSKI'S TRIUMPHS
OF NON-ANARCHICISED POETIC FORMS

Guillaume Apollinaire was something of a guru, not to say patron saint, for Czyżewski and the Polish futurists. Czyżewski's friend, Anatol Stern, even wrote a quirky, and comprehensive, biography of the great Polish-French poet.[27] Of course, there is nothing surprising in this. Even if Czyżewski hadn't spent some of his most formative years as an artist in Paris, it would be odd if, given his modernist predilections, he had *not* fallen under the strong influence of Apollinaire, who is without a doubt among the most talented, and influential, poets of the twentieth century.

Apollinaire's poetry is marked by inventive, playful and surrealistic (a term he coined) phrases such as *des troupeaux d'autobus mugissants près de toi roulent* [herds of mooing buses roll near you, 'Zone']. It is not difficult to find such striking combinations in Czyżewski's verse, such as that of the 'dog vomiting bullets' from 'Halfsleep' or the forks snoring and the knives drowsing in 'Dozing in the Café.' In 'Summer Evening,' the clouds 'crawl down from mountain tops' as if 'from caves.' And just as Apollinaire's narrator in 'Zone' expresses pious wonder for Christ *qui mont au ciel mieux que les aviateurs / Il déteint le record du monde pour la hauteur* ['who ascends the sky better than any aviator / Smashing the world record for altitude'], so Czyżewski peoples the sky above Kraków with futuristic angels in 'Lajkonik':

> The music plays — the people dance
> And sing.
> See the Lajkonik prance
> While, high above the city range
> Squadrons of angels in planes
> With wings of white,
> Leaping and bucking around
> The snares of clouds
> Sailing towards the sun.

The imagistic imagination — if we may risk misusing the term — is the same. Where Czyżewski differs from Apollinaire, in a formal sense, is his

---

27   Anatol Stern, *Dom Apollaire'a* (Kraków: Wydawnictwo Literackie, 1973).

training as a visual artist. We wish to take nothing away from Apollinaire as an acute appreciator of the visual arts, but it is one thing to assess a painting insightfully, and another to stand before a blank canvas and create something visually significant. We can see Czyżewski's remarkable sensitivity to visual forms in a verse like 'A Poem of Numbers.' In lines such as 'The family 141 / Going out for a stroll' we can almost see the unexpected allusion occurring to his mind as he looks at the numbers and sees the '4' between the two '1's almost like a child between his parents, swinging between them, suspended from their hands. And in the same poem, in the lines:

>The harmony of the waking soul
>   9   7   9

the harmony he writes of is his instinctual, immediate grasp of the geometric harmony of the numbers as a symmetrical succession of circle (9), incomplete triangle (7), and circle (9). This is something that cannot be taught, or, at least, will not be learned from dealing with words. Rather, it develops through long practice with the creation of visual communication. It is just like what Ezra Pound says of the sculptor Henri Gaudier-Brzeska:

> Gaudier Brzeska, who was accustomed to looking at the real shape of things, could read a certain amount of Chinese writing without ANY STUDY. He said, 'Of course, you can *see* it's a horse' (or a wing or whatever).[28]

Perhaps in verses like this, where he succeeds in 'anarchisising' mathematical symbols into anthropomorphic beings, or discovering to our eyes their deeper geometrical identities, Czyżewski comes closest to his creation of the autonomous poetic phrase. And here, we hasten to stress, the victory achieved is an intuitive one, which only a visual artist might grasp — it has nothing to do with theory *per se*. If it is not, as I suggest above, a case of 'two different authors,' one writing theory, and one composing verse, neither knowing anything of the other, then

---

28   Ezra Pound, *ABC of Reading* (New York: New Directions, 1960), p. 21

it becomes apparent that the poetry was written by Tytus Czyżewski the poet, and the theoretical manifestos by Tytus Czyżewski the painter.

Now, more in line with those programmatic writings, in which he refers to the use of onomatopoeia in primitive settings, is his frequent employment of sound-symbols stripped of any verbal ballast. For example, the transcription of the amorous alleycat in 'Alleycat Serenade' takes on the function of a rhyming refrain in that poem:

> Here in my room I sit and hear
> Curled near my lamp in the quiet
> His drawn out lubricious meow
>
> au   au   o - a - u

More subtle, and perhaps more poetically satisfying, is the manner in which the repetition of the word *springtime* in 'De Profundis' mimics the joyful pealing of bells:

> And my father following the plough
> spring following the plough
>   in the springtime springtime
> And my mother going to the fields
>   in the springtime springtime
> And the bells going to the fields
>   in the springtime springtime
> And all the birds fly to the fields
>   in the springtime springtime

It is sometimes said that, in his copious poetic output, Thomas Hardy never used the same verse-form twice. Considering his indubitable metrical brilliance, this exaggeration is well justified, and contains a good amount of truth. The same, I think, can be said for Czyżewski's inventiveness when it comes to poetic form. He is able to take even *banal speech* — literally — and turn it to striking poetic effect. Consider the following excerpt from 'The Regiment. A Military Romance:'

> the captain was pouring a drink
> the corporal was saluting

> the sergeant was saluting
> the lieutenant was passing by
> the lieutenant's fiancée was weeping
> **someone fired his Mauser**
> 2 soldiers went to get the coffin
> 2 soldiers were on guard duty
> 2 soldiers carried out the colonel
> the orderly carried round the orders

Here, the nearly washed-out progression of quotidian phrases masterfully gives back the ordinariness of even the greatest crimes of passion. Like Auden in his 'Musée des Beaux Arts' — but much more immediately, for where Auden describes, Czyżewski *shows* — the poet reveals to our eyes what all the uninterested parties were doing at the moment when the murderer ended the life of the adulterer… and then how, after this little blip in the routine, the world went on in its old, usual grooves. We are lulled asleep by the almost boring succession of banal descriptions until the bold and unexpected report of the gun startles us. And then, even before the echo dies away, we are soothed back into *le train-train quotidien* by the very next line, which pre-empts any deeper treatment of the dramatic, tragic event. Perhaps nowhere else in all of literature is our indifference to all suffering which is not our own, more strongly, more effectively, expressed.

'Expressionism' has various meanings when applied to the literature and the visual arts of the early twentieth century. As a matter of fact, the painter Czyżewski was associated with the Polish variety of this movement before he solidified the aesthetics of Formism. In literature, Expressionism is perhaps best represented by the haunting verses of his near contemporary and co-Austrian citizen, Georg Trakl. In verses both as peaceful as 'Musik im Mirabell' and as horrifying as 'Vorhölle' and 'Grodek,' the poet eschews the logical development of thought in favour of a collection of strong images, sometimes disparate ones, in an attempt at stirring in the soul of the reader a similar emotion to that which gripped him, the poet, at the composition of the poem in question. In poems like 'Fear,' Czyżewski also builds up a mood from subtle, repeated images, quite like Trakl. However, unlike the German-language poet, who is all about suggestion, Czyżewski explains perhaps too much, as here with the refrain-like 'fear takes possession of my mind.'

> In a dark and mealy-rotten wood
> Dusk falls on the thick limbs of trees
> (Fear takes possession of my mind)
> The shadow falls on yellow leaves
> The shadow falls on rusty moss
> (Through the sky there are birds that fly)
> (From the limbs there are leaves that fly)
> There is a black pool in the ancient wood
> The wind swept through the fields of wheat

The whole point of Expressionism is not to explain things, but to present them. Not to address the reader's mind with a transfer of information, but to appeal to the reader's emotions, allowing him or her, facilitating him or her, to experience on their own skin the phenomenon the poet wishes to convey. Czyżewski is more successful — if Expressionism is what he's aiming at — in a poem such as 'City. Autumn Evening:'

> *the tram sweeps off down the wide street*
> *cheeks with céruse are powdered white*
> *slippers are on the corpse's feet*
> *I smell the fresh scent of wet clay*
> *they beat the rugs on clothespoles hung*
> *mi fa so la si do re*
> *there's ladders rung after white rung*
> *in nurseries the babes are crying*
> *while clouds float slowly through the air*
> *the purples of the dawn are shining*
> *through the tatters of human despair*

or with the conclusion of 'The Assumption (An Idyll),' which is very Traklesque in the capturing of the present moment, the appeal to the senses:

> The cottage yards reek of manure...
> Roses cense the orchard trees
> Someone opens the tavern door
> A snatch of song flits on the breeze

Whether or not it's right to do so with as individual an artist as Czyżewski, literary historians, in their mania to classify, associate him with Futurism — as Zofia Ordyńska calls him 'the incontrovertible leader of the futurists.'[29] In poems such as 'Vision II,' Czyżewski adopts the imagery of the machine age as a fresh (then, though admittedly dated nowadays) vehicle for the expression of power, vitality:

> The brindled carrotty panther draws near
> Two shining arrows his electric eyes
> His brain acres-broad like a metro
> Black eyes each a pulsing dynamo
> Two wheels burning without fires
>
> *Oa*   *Oa*   *Oa*
> *R*   *R*   *R*

Here, futurism is very interestingly paired with the 'primitivism' of sound-poetry. In *The Snake, Orpheus and Eurydice* the anachronistic infixing of modernity, which characterises Czyżewski's brand of Futurism, is a brash confession of faith to the modern world:

> ORPHEUS
> — throws his lyre upon the ground —
> — the lyre — shatters —
> — a factory siren is heard in the distance —
> — the sun has set — from beyond the lake

Now, it is easy to chuckle at Futurism today, as the naive enthusiasm of early twentieth century man for the surges forward in technology just before, and after, the First World War — just as it is easy for us to deride the naïveté of Wordsworth's 'Steamboats, Viaducts and Railways' of a century earlier. But like the Romantic, who sensed the possible 'marring' of nature by man's 'lawful offspring,' so Czyżewski was no unqualified futuristic dreamer. It is somewhat chilling to read the summation of the first part of his 'self-criticism — selfadvertisement' of *The Green*

---

29 Zofia Ordyńska, *To już prawie sto lat: pamiętnik aktorki* (Wrocław: Ossolineum, 1970), p. 172.

Eye, with its prescient hedging of bets, from our twenty-first century perspective, when the unfavourable resolution of the 'either…or' clauses seems just around the corner:

> **'Electric Visions'** — a mechanised narrative poem.
> Man inseminated and unleashed the machine, which one day will either kill him, or **exalt** him.
> We build machines — we shall travel to the stars so as to observe the sun.
> The sun will marvel at where man found so much 'understanding.'
> Man will build a mechanical sun.
> The old sun — is an honest old machine.
> Let us love the sun and not talk about him behind his back.
> The man of the future is an electrical machine — sensitive, complicated, and simple in style.

Artists, like all people, are men and women of the times in which it has been given them to live. Czyżewski is no different. Whatever we may think of his 'futurism,' other references to twentieth-century culture are engaging. Such, for example, is his poetic enthusiasm for the cinema, and the faster-paced tempo of urban life, which spawned the hustle, organised crime, and the glorification thereof in *films noirs* and cheap detective novels. The form and diction of poems like 'Betrayal' accurately mirror these inspirations of the tenth muse:

> She went she felt she was with child
> She lay down on a sidewalk bench
> He grabbed his browning and he bit
> You bitch this is betrayal bitch

Likewise, 'She didn't know,' with its story of a girl beloved of two rivals (and its humorously innocuous turn, just when you expect jealous pistol shots to ring out) is a melodrama not much fit for the screen… but for all that, like 'The Regiment,' just the kind of domestic drama that happens time and again in this banal world.

There is a playfulness to much of the surreal in Czyżewski's poetry. It is interesting to set this side by side with the aesthetics of a friend and colleague of the poet. We are speaking of Leon Chwistek (1884–1944), another polymath (painter, aesthetician, professor of mathematics at Jagiellonian University). A close friend of Czyżewski's, in his *Wielość rzeczywistości w sztuce* [The Multiplicity of Realities in Art, 1924] Chwistek posited the existence of 'several, uncontradictory types of reality.' In the words of Agnieszka Morawińska:

> The two basic types of reality are the reality of sensory elements and the reality of things. These main concepts of reality, which are further subdivided, are represented in corresponding types of painting: the popular reality of things in primitive art, the physical reality of things in realism, the reality of sensations in Impressionism, the reality of ideas in Futurism and Formism. The last one is called by Chwistek the reality of visionaries.[30]

Although the play predates Chwistek's thesis by some fifteen years, something of the same openness to 'different' realities can be found in Czyżewski's first major literary work, the play *The Death of the Faun*. The peasant girls who first come across the pilgrim from the classical south flee him in fear. They see his horns and cloven hooves and take him for the devil. The sober-headed male peasants, wary of being taken advantage of by some sharp foreigner, try to figure out his angle. But it is the very fact of the physical appearance of a mythological figure in the reality of a Polish village that is shocking; it is as if one of the symbolist canvasses of Jacek Malczewski had suddenly come to life. The village priest is the most interesting of all of the characters, in that he speaks of the Faun, quite straightforwardly, as a 'woodland god' — without batting an eye at the obvious incompatibility of that statement with the uncompromising perspective of his monotheistic faith. It is as if parallel worlds could in fact exist, and two of them should somehow merge in this play; such is the nature of *this* reality that, quite logically, what was true *there* remains true *here*, even if that alien truth does not belong in this reality.

Thus, both the Faun and the Priest (especially the priest!) speak as if there were truth to the mythological story: the faun *actually does* reminisce about Horace, the priest *actually does* buy into the story of the Faun (fictional) and Horace (real) holding an actual conversation.

---

30   Morawińska, p. 45 (trans. Piotrowska).

> In this garden green, beside the fountain
> Sits Horace, musing
> At the foot of his mountain
> Soracte,
> Perusing
> A scroll. As a matter of fact, he's
> Having trouble
> With an ode for which he would
> Find the fittest metre; perhaps a double
> Cretic?
> That's all now, all he needs. And then his verse would go
> As smoothly as through soft black earth a hoe.
>
> PRIEST
> *(Caught off guard)*
> But how is it, Faun, that you speak our tongue?
> For you're from Roman legend, after all —
> And Horace, if I'm not mistaken, spoke
> To you in Latin?!... Hold on, I recall
> From my Poetics...

There is a charming tolerance to the attitude of the village rector here — although as the play develops, his amity with the unchristian, Dionysian being might spring more from his sense of superiority over his simpler parishioners than anything else— and after the murder of the Faun, he too, like the lord and lady of the manor, walks away, gets on with his day, leaving the corpse of his new friend there in the meadow, to be 'cleaned up' by someone else.

CZYŻEWSKI THE HUMANIST AND HIS PASTORALS

Of course, we needn't necessarily look for social criticism in this play, or in any of the works of Tytus Czyżewski. As Wat states in his memoirs, in reference to the entire group of formists and futurists:

> We were socially and politically cynical. We imaged socialism as, at bottom, the socialist doctrine, and the socialist ideal. [But] we understood our enemy to be collectivism — yes, that's

it — collectivism. Because that meant regulation, control; that was law. And we were about lawlessness.[31]

The anarchic attitude described by Wat does not, however, exclude empathy. In Czyżewski's 'Ode to Bread,' in which the staff of life is praised under elements as wide-ranging as the Host exposed in the monstrance for adoration, and the 'bread and butter' called for by peckish slicks in a 'Concertinocafé' we have this vignette of the suffering poor:

> When on a shaky table round which stand
> A group of children pale and underfed
> Each stretching toward the fresh round loaf a hand —
> While their mother slices thin the strong black bread
> In the dank crowded tenement basement
> Her mind drifts off to those not present…
> One girl sits at a cinema register
> Another rolls cigars throughout the day
> A third's out hawking the Evening Courier
> A fourth one walks the streets to earn her pay…

Anatol Stern states that the Futurists wore the term of opprobrium 'bolsheviks,' which was tossed a them by the disapproving traditionalists at the appearance of their first manifesto, as a badge of honour.[32] It is doubtful that Czyżewski was political in this sense, at least judging from *Robespierre* and its robust critique of totalitarianism, not to mention the forceful description of some of the key words found there: 'Nation and Freedom and a word slimy with pus like a wound / Revolution.' No, Czyżewski's empathy arises from a deeper well, that of basic human solidarity. And here we may mention the 'pastorals.'

For Czesław Miłosz, it seems as if these festive works were the be-all and end-all of Czyżewski's poetic output. In his *History of Polish Literature*, the pastorals make up the entirety of the entry devoted to the poet-painter:

---

31   Wat, p. 28.
32   Stern, p. 16.

> [...] Valued today as a painter, [Czyżewski] was also a poet, and his works have a right to a place in every anthology. Tytus Czyżewski wrote very little, but his *Pastorals* (*Pastorałki*, published in Paris in 1925), for instance, are of great beauty. [...] In these naïve and purposely awkward Christmas carols he gave an avant-garde treatment to motifs from old Polish poetry [...] As an avant-garde poet he completely rejected nineteenth-century metrics; he was able, thus, to invent new verse instrumentation for old melodies.[33]

As we have seen, there is a lot more to Czyżewski than just the pastorals, many of which — like the 1586 *Dialog na Boże Narodzenie* [Christmas Dialogue] or the 1648 *Actus pastoralis* — are recreations of the old Renaissance traditions of the Christmas play, and not mere 'carols.' One might also question Miłosz's assertion of Czyżewski writing 'very little' — surely a relative term. Whatever the case may be, it is certain that the pastoral genre fascinated the poet, and that his works of this type form an important segment of his poetic *oeuvre*. But why on earth did he write so many?

It goes without saying that Czyżewski, who survived the First World War just to die as the cataclysm of the Second was coming to an end, lived in tumultuous, horrifying times. Perhaps his penchant for the stillness and peaceful promises of Christmas can be partially explained by the desire — both conscious and subliminal — for peace and charity in the soul of one whose fate it was to live amidst so much anxiety and hatred, in an age which saw his prophecy of the machine coming to horrid fruition in mechanised war and Blitzkrieg. We have already mentioned the inclusive nature of these works, in which Slovakia is recognised as just as constituent, and native, an element of the mountainous region radiating out from the charmingly-located manger as Poland. What a sorrow it must have been for him in 1939, to see the troops of Monsignor Tiso's Slovakia invade Poland from the south, as allies of Hitler's Germany...

Czyżewski is not a confessional poet. The pastorals — both dramatic and hymnic — are the only Christian poems in the repertoire

---

33 Czesław Miłosz, *History of Polish Literature* (Berkeley: University of California Press, 1983), pp. 400-401.

of the great avant-gardist. However, Christian themes are easy to find sprinkled throughout the poems and plays; we will point out just one, as it bears on the topic at hand, Czyżewski's mastery of form. Amidst all the seemingly absurd enumerations of phenomena that make up the poem 'Night – Day,' suddenly, the poem concludes with a reference to the most absurd — and paradoxically most meaningful — event in history: the death of God on the Cross:

	SPARKS	
burn	abrade	explode
and day		smoulders
and night		crows
	NAILS	
bleed	weep	cross

We are not prepared for the sudden shift, and the last four words hit us with extraordinary force. It is as if the poet lulled us to sleep with his assessment of the absurdity of the world, only to grab us by the collar and roughly shake us before the central event, which gives sense to everything.

THE AVANT-GARDE THEN, AND NOW

One of the most curious things concerning the splendid phenomenon of Tadeusz Kantor is his insistence on being classified an avant-garde artist. For most historians of art, the term is particularly appropriate when applied to the artists and ideas emanating from Paris in the early decades of the twentieth century, when — following the world-changing events ushered in by the First World War — we saw an almost complete break with the artistic traditions of the past (Hugo Ball) or at least a complete break with the traditional modes of expressing the past (Ezra Pound, T.S. Eliot). At the time when, for example 'The Love Song of J. Alfred Prufrock' was published, Kantor was two years old. What makes Kantor an avant-garde artist above all is his devotion to the ideals espoused by the post-World War I generation, which directly preceded his own. This is not hard to understand. He came into his first serious phase as a young artist during the Nazi occupation of Kraków, and, after the defeat of Germany by the Allies, there was no liberation for Poland. One (brown) totalitarianism was replaced by another — the red totalitarianism of Soviet hegemony, which — especially during the early fifties — weighed heavily upon the free expression of artists until its overthrow, beginning in Poland, in 1989. Throughout all these years Kantor, his art and his theatre, were subjected to various forms of repression or neglect by the powers that were. The avant-garde for him, then, is an energetic assertion of artistic liberty, the individuality of the artist, the artist's right to follow the directives of his muse, wherever she will lead him, whatever anyone else has to say about that.

We have been speaking of Tytus Czyżewski in reference to what was happening around him — the rise of Formism and Futurism, in which he played so central a role — and in reference to the shoulders upon which he stood — in particular, those of Guillaume Apollinaire. It is just as important to note, albeit briefly, Czyżewski's influence on the present.

We have already noted that Kantor, arguably the most inventive and recognised Polish artist of the second half of the twentieth century, attended the lectures of Tytus Czyżewski in pre-war Kraków, where he was a student. The Cricot Theatre, which Kantor was to reanimate and reinvigorate after the war, was, along with the Bagatela Theatre, one of the primary venues for the production of Czyżewski's dramas, and certain figures of Cricot — especially Maria Jarema — form a living link between the pre-war avant-garde Cricot, and Kantor's Cricot 2. One of the first plays staged by Cricot 2 was *The Death of the Faun* (7 VI 1945), with scenography and costumes by Tadeusz Kantor. Czyżewski's influence on Kantor is unquestionable. When one considers such scenes from the later 'spectacula' of Cricot 2 as the description of the actors at the outset of *Umarła klasa* [The Dead Class, 1975]:

> Perhaps they are WAX FIGURES,
> masterfully similar to living people. Some stand in front, looking steadfastly at the entering crowd, as if they were searching for someone; others are frozen in the half-movement of rising from the bench; still others are leaning out to see better, looking over the shoulders of those in front, with an expression of anticipation frozen on their faces, an expression of patience, of patient endurance ...
> They stand like this until all of the spectators have entered and taken their seats...

Abased, somehow, they have been put on display:
like the condemned ...
No, more: like the DEAD.
From the very first moment when the audience enters the theatre, a sensation of
D i v i s i o n should be created:
equivocally — a sensation simultaneously repulsive and attractive,
a being drawn to the terrible endurance of this inhuman immobility,
similar to t h e d e a d!
'On the other side!':
The benches as catafalques.
A CLOSET OF WAX FIGURES.
ILLUSION!

or the marriage scene in *Wielopole, Wielopole* (1980):

FATHER begins to move his legs. Makes mistakes. Becomes discouraged. 'Dies' again — and tries again. Thus, with difficulty, does he make his way over to the edge of the stage, to the edge of the Room.
The PRIEST goes on marching with his Cross. He's right before the audience. He swings his arm with fervour, in time to the march. Throws his legs out in front of him. Satisfied. Wholly transformed into this MARCH. Finally, he takes the cross from his shoulder and sets it down upon a chair as if he'd just recalled something. He goes out to the antechamber where the body of the dead BRIDE lies in her wedding dress.
Completely white.
He lifts her up, drags her, takes the stiff form into his arms, and sets her up next to FATHER like a doll[34]

---

34 Translations from the theatrical works of Tadeusz Kantor are my own. In 1993-1994 I translated all of Kantor's theatrical works into English at the Cricoteka Archives. Unfortunately, because of the intransigence of certain parties, they remain unpublished. However, they are regularly used and cited by foreign scholars of Kantor's works, who cannot access the Polish originals.

it is hard not to posit the source of Kantor's fascination with mannequins, and the staccato speech-patterns of the long-dead, revivified in memory, in such otherworldly scenes as this, from *A Burglar of the Better Sort*:

> *From his place along the side wall, the mannequin (the Ingénieur du Métropolitain) moves toward the centre of the stage, with wooden strides. The clock strikes twelve again. A shimmy begins to spill out of the great horn of the gramophone at the front of the stage — the rooster crows three times*
>
> MÉTROPOLITAIN
> *(walking about the stage with wooden strides, in time to the beat of the music and the tones of the striking clock)*
>   One   two   three
>   mon   sieur   gawks   at   ma   dame
> 'tis   I   that   built   le   Mé   tro   po   li   tain
>   Deep   un   der   Pa   ris
>   hop   hop   hop
>
> *(The music stops playing)*
> *The burglar and the guest assume the movements of the mannequin*
> *(The music begins to play)*

The circular dances in this play, too — how similar to Kantor's repetitive Argentinian tangos, or the parade of the actors behind the triumphant Whore/Death near the conclusion of *Niech szczezną artyści* [Let the Artists Croak, 1985]. Similarly, the repetitions of the rooster crowing and the clock striking, not to mention the sudden reanimation — but in a different sort of existence? — of characters we thought were dead, were all to become hallmarks of Kantor's theatre — especially the last-named spectaculum, with its expanding of temporality into eternity, its monumental mixing of past and present, like jumbled photographic negatives superimposed on one another.

    Whom Czyżewski will spur to creation in the future is unknown. But future heirs there will be; his poems, plays, and paintings will be relevant as long as there exists an artistic impulse to unfettered, unafraid, self expression.

ON THIS TRANSLATION

This translation is based on the exquisitely and lovingly produced edition of Czyżewski's poems and dramatic works edited by the poets Janusz Kryszak and Andrzej K. Waśkiewicz, which, is, and promises to be for many years, the definitive collection of the poet's literary works. Our translation differs from the original in the arrangement of the texts. Kryszak and Waśkiewicz divide the book into two uneven halves, the first consisting of the poems and the second of the dramatic works. Their rationale is as follows:

> The arrangement of the works as proposed by us entails that the poet's first published work is presented after works from the late 1930s. This disrupts the actual order of his evolution as a writer. But any other established chronology is, at the present state of research, impossible [... But] further uncertainties are introduced by the fact that, in the case of Czyżewski, the execution of a strict demarcation between 'lyrical' and 'dramatic' works is practically impossible.[35]

We can only applaud the delicacy with which the editors have approached the matter of chronology. Still, one wonders if the 'demarcation' between what is poetry, and what is a 'dramatic work,' is not as arbitrary as the demarcation of literary periods. After all, they hint to this themselves. *Robespierre* is, for all intents and purposes, like *Lajkonik*, a dramatic work, although it is included in a publication that includes lyric poetry. *The Death of the Faun*, indubitably a work meant for the stage, includes a very proper elegy expounded by the Faun lazing on the bright forest clearing, and reminiscing on his interactions, long ago in BC, with Quintus Horatius Flaccus. In our translation, unencumbered by the exigencies of scholarship, we cut the Gordian knot and present the works in order. Whether *Donkey and Sun in Metamorphosis* was produced before the publication of *Night — Day* (both works are from 1922) is, in the broad scheme of things, irrelevant. Tytus Czyżewski isn't

---

35   Kryszak and Waśkiewicz, p. 326.

magically transformed from poet to dramatist on 13 August, when he completes his work on his newest volume of poetry, and then sets out to write his next theatrical piece. Poetic creation is not a chicken-and-egg phenomenon. Creative work, whatever its (arbitrary) genre, gestates in the poet's soul simultaneously with other projects. There may be — there probably ought to be — a difference between the output of a given poet, say, in 1985, and that of 2015, but any stricter chronological order is not only impossible, it is senseless and counterproductive. We depart, therefore, from the order of texts as presented by Kryszak and Waśkiewicz, and order the works of Tytus Czyżewski, regardless of genre, in a progression, which, we believe, allows the reader a clearer grasp of the poet's evolution.

As far as the translation itself is concerned, I have little here to add to what I have already espoused in earlier publications. Form is also content, and a poet's form is to be respected by the translator as faithfully as the ideas he expresses. When dealing with a poet like Czyżewski, to whom form is crucial, when (and if) it comes to a conflict between verbatim renditions of the 'ideological content' and faithfulness to the form of his expression, it must be the latter that guides the translator.

One brief example of this may be given. In *The Snake, Orpheus and Eurydice,* a group of boys bearing baskets of grapes crosses the stage. They sing the following ribald song:

> bacchus bacchus
> you limp asparagus
> what have you done you clown,
> spilling your seed on the ground.
>
> You silly jackanapes
> sowing for pumpkins and grapes
> while orchard and rose are red
> and we've wreaths upon the head.
>
> In the olive grove nearby
> there's sweet smelling moss and grass,
> how sweet it is, old boy, to lie
> there, couched upon a naked lass.

This would give back in English the following lines:

> bachusie, bachusie
> ty wstrętny wisusie
> coś ty narobił nieboże
> że już posiałeś zboże.
>
> Że już posiałeś zboże,
> dynie i winogrady,
> już kwitną róże i sady
> i wieniec włożę na głowę.
>
> W oliwnym gaju przy drodze
> są mchy miękkie woniące
> jak mile jest tam spanie
> z nagą dziewczyną kochaną.

The above is, to paraphrase Eugene A. Nida, an example of dynamic translation, which seeks to arouse in the reader of the translation a comparable reaction to that of the reader of the original, sacrificing, if need be, a pedantic faithfulness to the letter. The classic example of this is a translator rendering the Biblical 'white as snow' as 'white as egret feathers,' when the audience he is appealing to comes from a climate where snow has never been seen. It is not the snow that is important, but the blinding purity of colour. A 'literal' translation of these lines — if one were possible — would read something like this:

> Bacchus, Bacchus
> you horrid scamp
> what have you done, poor thing
> that you've already sown the wheat.
>
> That you've already sown the wheat
> the pumpkins and the grapes
> and roses and orchards are already blossoming
> and I set a wreath upon my head.

> In the olive orchard near the road
> there are mosses soft and fragrant.
> How sweet it is to sleep there
> with a dear, naked girl.

Nida's translator was faced with the choice: Do I replicate the immediacy of 'shocking, pure white' to the reader of my translation, or do I persist in a verbatim faithfulness to the original text, and speak of something being as 'white as snow' to an audience, whose only experience is tropical humidity? I think we can all agree that he made the right decision here, in choosing egret feathers; it was a poetic choice, not a scholarly one, and what the text 'loses' in pedantic faithfulness to the letter, it gains, or at least retains, in poetic immediacy.

Our decision is identical. In choosing to translate the bawdy waggishness of the boys' song, with its quick rhymes, jaunty metre and erotic subtexts, rather than opting for lexical accuracy where it didn't fit (*wisus*, which can be approximated as 'scamp,' is an archaic word, seldom used today) we convey to the reader — I hope — the fact that Tytus Czyżewski was a poet.

The translator of poetry is more medium than scholar. He must allow himself to be possessed by the spirit of the original poet, and transmit, in the target language, the vital poetic plasma of the original. He must recreate the original poem as if the original poet were writing in the target language. In this case, Tytus Czyżewski would still be aiming at ribald, Villonesque diction, and 'scamp' would never occur to him in the context of finding rhymes for 'Bacchus.' When the translator of verse fails at this task, he commits a greater treason to the original poet than mere word-approximation.

ACKNOWLEDGEMENTS

This translation was completed during a residency at the Translators' Collegium of the Book Institute of Poland in Kraków, during the summer of 2019. I am deeply grateful to everyone at the Book Institute for their continued support of my translations, including the grant that made the publication of this book possible, and especially for the invaluable period of undisturbed peace in the most congenial surroundings, in which the lion's share of my work was carried out. My thanks are also due to Glagoslav Publications, and my editor Ksenia

Papazova, for their continued enthusiasm for the dissemination of Polish literature in English.

Jak zawsze, tę książkę poświęcam mojej Oli.

Charles S. Kraszewski
Kraków, 15 July 2019

The Death of the Faun

A Little Picture

(1907)

Persons:

FAUN, AN OLD WOODLAND GOD
OLD PARISH PRIEST
LORD OF THE MANOR
LADY OF THE MANOR
ORGANIST
VILLAGE ALDERMAN[36]
HIRED-HAND …
OLD WOMAN
GIRL I
GIRL II
SHEPHERD — PEASANTS — OLD WOMEN — GIRLS — HIRED HANDS

The action takes place in the spring, in the depths of a distant village.

Wandering through the woods, a certain old Faun — lonely — yearning for life and fun — arrived one day at the outskirts of a Polish village. Sun — forest aromas — life and love all around him — these set the old Faun to dreaming. Warming himself in the sun — he thinks back upon the days of his youth — He sighs from time to time, complains, bewailing his old age and his loneliness.

But all the same he's still a wisecracker, jocose; from time to time he gets the urge to belch fearsomely — to give the girls singing about the woods a proper fright, or maybe to tempt them near. Because — as the

---

36 Please refer to the Notes section at the end of the book for definitions of unfamiliar terms, textual explanations, and contextual notes.

saying goes — 'despite his age he still can rage.' Hearing his bellows, the girls rush into the clearing. Catching sight of his big shaggy frame, they think he's the devil — and rush off to the village to spread the word. What happened next, and how, and what came of it all — the action about to commence will discover.

Early morning — woods. A green clearing, bathed in springtime sunlight. The dark green wood casts its shadows at the edge of the clearing. Thick green grass, here and there white, yellow and pink flowers blooming. Birdsong is heard from the forest. Sometimes, the wind stirs the dark branches of the firs... Sometimes a cuckoo sounds... It is quiet and calm in the golden-green clearing.
Once and again, a song from the woods is heard.
That voice spreads its echoes through the woods and dies away.
The voice of a young girl is heard in the distance...

> SONG
> The cuckoo's kook- kook- kooking
> For her ma and pa she's looking.
> *(Pause)*
> Hey, deep in the earth they lie.
> Hey, they cannot hear you cry,
> > hu, ha!

> *(Silence)*
> *(After a while, the voice of another girl, nearer the clearing, is heard)*

> SONG
> Hey there little green meadow,
> Hey there field lush with grass,
> On a grey horse Janosik is riding,
> Riding to me, his lass.
> > hu, ha!

(The echoes die away in the forest, and quiet ensues)
(The old, stoop-shouldered Faun wanders out of the wood and into the clearing. He pricks his ears, stretches, looks up at the sun)

FAUN
Green growth covers the leas,
It smells of herbs —
All of nature seethes
With sun!
From the village, some singing
Wafts, or from the wood;
The songs of the Dryads?
The woodland Nymphs?
Maybe it's them that's howling.
In my younger days, long ago
After them I'd hunting go,
In the barefoot Dryads' paces —
How much pleasure in those chases!
O, I'd give a chalice full of wine —
Today, when I've burned through my youthful days,
Only the sun warms this exhausted hide.
I can only peep at love now,
Lurking near a peasant's window.
Sitting here in the thickets
Sometimes I see,
Some boy and girl embracing,
Some goat after nanny chasing,
Or mating marten, mating fox,
Or in the stream among the rocks
The fishes rubbing, flashing
Scales in the sun…
. . . .

(*Song again, from the depths of the woods*)
The wind it blows, the wind it blows
The woods sigh in the wind
— — — — — — —
Whoever knows, whoever knows
Where my Jasiecek's been
        hu, ha!

FAUN
O, how she's singing that tune!
Tempting the fly into the snare?
— — — — — —

(Slowly at first, in melancholic strains, then with passion)

She's lain her down among the flowers
She's plucked a flower, and waves
Away the heat that scorches, burns
Even there in the shade;
She hums, she sings
Calling, tempting,
'Come to me here among the thickset ferns;
Come, use my body that for loving yearns —
Taste my hot blood
Then in your shaggy arms
Carry me, racing through the wood;
Come, taste of my trembling charms
And never let me catch my breath,
Never from frenzy let me rest —
See how I bend my head and rake
My hair across the herb-thick brake;
Rush me into the darkest forest thicket...'
. . . .
(Pause)
That was a vision of delight,
A dream of love, a wondrous dream —
The slightest murmur sets to flight
That kind of dream, the vision of my spring...

(Silence — the forest rustles lazily — a song from afar:)

Cry not my love, O, what's the matter?
Weep not, my sweet raspberry.
Your lover must his horses water;
This only makes him tarry.

(A voice nearer the clearing)

He'll come for sure, he'll come tonight,
There's nothing yet to rue.
And when he's taken his delight
My girl, why, you'll come too!
         hu ha!
. . . .

FAUN
Eh — those are the village girls
In red skirts and yellow kerchiefs,
It's them that's howling through the woods
I thought — —
I thought it was them, from my own springtime —
I came across one of these, once,
Stupid! She ran away with such a yell:
The devil! The devil!
— — — — — — —
Maybe we ought to have some fun with them,
Make them shiver:
(Loudly:)
Meh — e — e — ehh!...

(Pause. Then a girl comes out of the forest, stands, gazes — the sun is against her, so she shields her eyes — then in wonder — in terror — she makes the sign of the Cross and runs back into the wood, with a scream)

FAUN
Well, if that's how she reacts,
I'll belch again:
Beh — e — e — ehh!...
. . . .

(From the woods, the girls calling: Maryś! Jaguś! Kasiu!)
(A moment of silence. The sun is beating down still more strongly — from time to time a soft rustle can be heard from the wood.)
(The Faun lies down on the ground to warm himself in the sun. Pause)

O fiery sun
How you burn
— — — — — — —

(Melancholy)
How scorching the blaze
The sparks flash on the streams
The olive orchards in the swelter laze
The peach orchard gleams
With golden fruit; mulberry trees
Half-green pant for a breeze…
In this garden green, beside the fountain
Sits Horace, musing
At the foot of his mountain
Soracte,
Perusing
A scroll. As a matter of fact, he's
Having trouble
With an ode for which he would
Find the fittest metre; perhaps a double
Cretic?
That's all now, all he needs. And then his verse would go
As smoothly as through soft black earth a hoe.
Sometimes above his book
He lifts his eye to have a look
Upon the fields stretching afar like a smear;
At slender poplar and thick yew;
At how the hazy hills seem to disappear
Into the blue.
And the old man dreams,
And the gods reawaken, it seems,
Forest and sapphire field,
Streams of crystal water yield
Ancient deities
— There are fanfares among the trees —
Diana sets her hounds
At the lascivious stag
Who flees, and vainly bounds
Down through the valley to the stream,

But there he's cornered by the gang
Of dogs that pounce on him
With claw and fang;
They bite, they tear, they drag…
And there, upon that pasture white
With blossoms, a grey flock of sheep;
Watch over them a shepherd keeps.
That's Phoebus, god of light,
God of the sure arrow's flight.
He's led his flock out onto the meadows
And, lute in hand, he slowly goes
Strumming —
What's that gay riot coming,
Dancing here, nearing us?
Bacchus!
In green of the vine, green of the lawn;
Around him shriek and whistle the raucous Fauns.
The drunken Muses dance,
And fat Silenus claps his hands
And laughs — the echo
Wakens the forests as they go
Wide spreading; the Fauns prance,
Merry with wine; a fiery glance
Darting on all sides,
Their lusty songs rebounding far and wide…
Such is a poet, dreaming
Of gods and suns and flowery meads gleaming,
Until the drowsy buzz of bees
Above his head lulls him to drowse… now he's…
Asleep… cool in the shade of the trees'
Dark limbs;
Above him, on whooshing wings, a white cloud swims — —
— — — — — — — — —
(Pause)
(The footsteps and voices of a crowd of people resound from the wood — the Faun pricks his ears)
(Onto the clearing, from the wood, comes the Priest in his surplice — the Organist with aspergillum and holy water — followed by a crowd

of peasants — hired hands — girls — and women with hoes slung over their shoulders — all of these stand at the edge of the clearing — looking around)

FAUN
(Looking their way)
What is this group of people?
Is it Faunalia today?

PRIEST
Well, where is he?
Silly woman, spreading panic!
Where is this devil?

GIRL
I saw him standing right here!
With horns just like a goat,
And cloven goats' feet too, stamping,
And shaggy — all over — but he's
Very old. Among those old pine trees
I came, and heard a roaring —
I peeped out, and right before me
I saw him sitting, right
There — I nearly died of fright!

HIRED HAND KUBA
Sure, and Once Upon a Time...
Some spirit there was, for sure —
Elderberry wine!
What sort of self-respecting demon
Would choose this dump to be seen in?

SOME OLD WOMAN
(From among the crowd, shouting)
O Jesus — something's moving over there!
Is that himself, the devil — !

PEOPLE
Where, where —...?

OLD WOMAN
There, O, under the fir!

(Now everyone sees the Faun, and are gripped with fright — the Priest and Organist approach him with trepidation — the frightened people bless themselves — and draw back)

PRIEST
(Approaches the Faun — in a trembling voice)
Exorciso te in...

FAUN
(Rising)

I am a faun,
A woodland god.
I'm from a classical country.
These silly wenches, I reckon,
Told you of me.
I'm quite exhausted with age.
But now, by the spring sun
Warmed to the marrow of my bones,
Old memories awaken,
Memories of my younger days.
I dream...

PRIEST
(Dumbfounded)
What? Are you that Faunus, then,
Of whom the ancient poets sing?
Aha — It's coming back to me — — —
You lived in Hellas, lived in Rome,
And now you've wandered O so far from home —
And without fear?
But why have you come here?!

Was it some conjurer enticed
You? Or some artist, wanting you to pose?
That you're no devil, everybody knows.
Today he goes about in a different disguise:
I've proof canonical, as far as that goes.

FAUN
From the Italian lands I have come here,
For all the other Fauns have died
And all the Nymphs have disappeared.
Dryads to mortal girls transmogrified,
And now I'm speeding down the shady slope
Of time.
And so I wander through the woods in hope
Of finding any old friend of mine.

PRIEST
(Caught off guard)
But how is it, Faun, that you speak our tongue?
For you're from Roman legend, after all —
And Horace, if I'm not mistaken, spoke
To you in Latin?!… Hold on, I still recall
From my Poetics… I can still remember…
Hold on… Aha…
(Declaims)
Faune, Nympharum fugientum amator
per meos fines et aprica rura
lenis incedas abeasque parvis
Aequus Alumnis…
si tener pleno cadit haedus anno
larga nec desunt Veneris sodali
vina craterae, vetus ara multo
fumat odore.
. . . .
And then it ends with:
Inter audaces lupus errat agnos…
Hold on… I can't quite remember the end…

...It's Latin after all — but tell me, how
You understand our speech — ?!

FAUN
Walking through the woods and fields here,
I've grown accustomed to your tongue;
The peasant, ploughing, chatters to the soil,
The shepherd to his flock, when they're out grazing,
The maiden in the woods — to the spring sun
They sing
The trees sigh
The brooks whisper
In your language
You Barbari —
The earth here too, when the storm lashes it,
Complains aloud in your speech,
Was it from the earth that you learned to speak,
You Barbari?!...
What country is this?
(To the priest)
And who might you be?!

PRIEST
I am the rector of the parish here.
I teach the folk, and root out all their vices:
Impurity, insobriety, theft,
And suchlike swinishness.
I snip short arrogance, I settle quarrels
Between the manor and the people;
This wood of common fir trees
Belongs to our lord of the manor,
A lovely fellow —
Great lover of the arts and your homeland
Italy — he loves art — he often goes there
And then he writes it all down in his memoirs
So that the whole nation benefits.
O, 'cos we've a long way to go yet
Until our nation's culture catches up

With that of foreign parts — as for this country,
It's gained a scar or two in roustabouts — —
Unnecessary quite — but famous, ho!
They're written up in histories, in fact.
But it's an ordinary little country:
Crows have their nests here,
Magpies, storks and such —
Its name — Polonia.

FAUN
Aha — Polonia — you're Poloni.
I've heard something of you.
It seems you're quite thin-skinned
When it comes to what others say of you,
Sick for their praise... But jolly all the same:
Supposedly, you like to dance and drink,
A lot. But that's all I know about you
— I was busied with myself,
My life... When the grapes mature,
Where the most beautiful Dryad is to be found —
What key the starling sings in, or the woodpecker...
I thought of this,
For this I lived.
O man, can you even imagine
Me — for whom the forest hummed with life;
Me — for whom each corner of the woods
Shivered ecstatically —
Me, the carefree, sprightly Faun...
(Pause)
And now look:
Old age — like a Gorgon, evil...
Look! My beard falls out in patches —
My horns askew, nearly falling from my brow!
Just look what I've come to!
I who lived for beauty and love alone —
Look what I've come to!
(Buries his face in his hands)
— — — — — — —

(Meanwhile, ever more people arrive — old women, hired hands, girls — they gather round the Faun, gaping)
(The Village Alderman arrives in haste)

VILLAGE ALDERMAN
Praised be Jesus Christ…!
Good morning, Reverend Father.
(He kisses the Priest's hand)

PRIEST
…Forever and ever, amen.
How are you, Alderman?

VILLAGE ALDERMAN
(Greatly surprised)
Why, here I've come a-runnin', Reverend Father —
I'm ploughing up the field not far from here,
And a wench comes up running,
Spoutin' about sommat' in the woods,
An' so I come a-runnin'
Like the devil fleein' Holy Wa—
. . . .
An' what on earth is that?
Some unclean potentate?
Is that a costyume? Or what?!

PRIEST
It's a poor old Faun
From the Italian lands.

VILLAGE ALDERMAN
It's an ugly fawn you got there!
If that's a fawn, I'd like to see the doe…
(He looks at him more carefully. Astonished, he shakes his head)
…Or maybe not…
Maybe it's just a tramp?
Maybe we should let the officers know
Because now…

PRIEST
Eh no, no.
Eh — you see, it's like,
How can I explain it to you…
This is an ancient god in a strange form.
I'll tell you all about it
Some other time.
Because even a man — you know, can become distorted…

VILLAGE ALDERMAN
Eh — mebbe it's that Andy Christ.
'Cos in the papers they said
The end of the world is a-comin'.

HIRED HAND KUBA
Eh, this one here,
That's a prestifrigerator.
A bum in fancy-dress
Who wantsa play a commodity.
Devil? — Pshaw!
When I was in Germany Gastarbitin'
I saw a mug just like his.
In a certain town
Same as him
But made of iron or tin
Sittin' in a fountain
Spoutin'
Water from his mug. —

ORGANIST
Kuba stop your jabbering
About things of what you're ignorant.
This is… ah, but you wouldn't understand it if I told you.
(Looks around)
Look look, how many people're here!
It's the whole village, I reckon!

PRIEST
Now what're you all gaping at?
Back to work! You get paid
For catching flies with your mouth?

(He chases them off — just as a Girl comes running up into the clearing, breathless)

GIRL
Father! Father! Reverend Father!
Krasula's calving
An' it's a hard one.
They can't handle it by themselves.
The housekeepers are calling,
They want you to come.
— — — — — — — — —
They can't handle it by themselves.
It's a preach birth!

PRIEST
Quiet, you stupid girl.
I'll be right along.
    (To Faun)
And you Faun, stay right here.
I'll be right back.

FAUN
Don't go! — Who'll I have to talk to?
These people?
I want to tell you
All about my sadness.
I want to tell you all about my woe.
Get it all out,
Get it all off my chest.
Don't go!
You're leaving me here alone with these peasants,
This rabble!

HIRED HAND KUBA
    (Irate)
Well, see that now? See!
You cow-horny faker you!
That's enough of that rabble talk!
We're a noble nation, now!
Bugger off to where you've come from.
There's nothing for you here —
An' just you try to take it!
(Makes a fist in anger)
'Cos when I wallop you,
Those horns o' yours'll fly off to the knacker's
Where you stoled 'em!

PRIEST
What's going on?
Calm down, calm down!
You think you're in a tavern?

HIRED HAND KUBA
Well it ain't his local!
We don't want no furriners here!

PRIEST
    (To Faun)
I'll be coming back here soon —
I'll take you to the rectory.
You'll spend the night there with me.

OLD WOMAN
Eh, that ain't wise your Reverence —
That sorta goblin in the house!
'E's like the very devil painted
In the church
— No 'ffence intended…
Just like the devil on the wall
Who's fricasseein' souls in Hell.
Or t'other with the bellows

Keepin' the flames hot
Beneath the sooty pot.
But if that's what your Reverence druthers,
Well then…

PRIEST
Is it your business? Quiet!
    (To the Organist)
You stay here and make sure
No harm comes to him from these boors.
I'll be right back!

(Another Girl runs up, yelling)

GIRL II
Father, Father,
The cook's sent me —
You've got company!

PRIEST
What? Who's come?

GIRL II
The lord of the manor himself, it seems —

PRIEST
I'm on my way.
I wonder what he'll have to say…
Things like this don't happen every day…
    (He exits hurriedly)

(The Faun gets up — stretches — gazes up at the sun. The sun rises higher in the sky — bathing the clearing in light — burning hot. Meanwhile, the people inch closer to the Faun — old women, hired hands, peasants and village shepherds — This one touches his horns, that one gives a pull on his hair — then shyness gives way to bold jollity, which takes possession of them all at the sight of the funny creature)

VILLAGE ALDERMAN
If you weren't so old
I'd've said you were playin' dress-up.
Like those horns, those hooves
      (Takes the former in hand, looks at the latter)
Were part of a costume — for fun.
— — — — — — — — —
      (Scratching his head, he shakes it)
But bugger me if you're not really such a one!

OLD WOMAN
Let'm alone — he must be some sorta milord
If Father's even invited him in.
Well, nothing can surprise me any more.
And every body lives on his own score.

HIRED HAND KUBA
Eh — he's some sorta comedian
Who plays pretend.
I'll ask him if he's married.
    (To Faun)
Hey you — you got a woman?

FAUN
What did he say?

ORGANIST
He's asking if you're married.

FAUN
Married? He's asking if I have a wife?
I've practised free love all my life
And I've been loved
By goddesses of great beauty.
In shady copses they've sung to me
Songs of delight,
And then we'd
Dance ourselves into a frenzy,

Laughing and chasing through the green forests.
And then came the fevered night,
When body tight to body pressed...
And then we'd slake our thirst
With the black fruit of the vine,
Our sense immersed
        — in wine!

ORGANIST
Wine — O I have wine...
        (Pulls from his pocket a little bottle)
Good altar wine, not watered down.
The same the lord of the manor drinks
When he comes a-visiting
To the rectory...
I was to take this to the church, in fact...

(The Faun grabs the bottle — takes a deep draught — the people are scandalised — some of them stretch out their arms — making as if to rush upon him with their fists — the Organist blocks their way)

VILLAGE ALDERMAN
        (Scandalised)
Eh verger, now that wasn't right
To let him drink that altar wine!
That's blasphemy
To give the wine that's meant for Mass
To such a shaggy old jackass.

PEOPLE
That's right, that's right, you wait and see —
You're tempting the Lord's punishment,
And Reverend Father will be mad.

ORGANIST
Ah, people — calm down!
The Reverend Father needn't know!

Let the old fellow have a nip
Of nourishment.

FAUN
>(Drinks again — a little drunk, he begins to declaim, and his declamation turns into song and dance)

O drink divine of Dionysus!
Thou soakest these old bones with strength!
Again I feel that I'm a Faun!
My muscles, like young panthers, spry,
My legs are strong enough to fly!
Evoe Liber god, he — ha —
The drink divine swims in my brains;
My bones are strangely strong again —
Now how I'd race among the trees
Coursing, with thee, after fillies,
Evoe Liber god, he ha!
But now I'd dance a little round
With cloven hoof stomping the ground,
Leading in dance Terpsichore
If someone'd pipe a tune for me!
I still can dance; I still can prance;
My drunken feet can thump the sod!
He ha, evoe Liber god...

(The people are taken by surprise, then they laugh — and a general gaiety spreads through their ranks, growing more and more)

HIRED HAND KUBA
He's not a half-bad dancer, eh?
But he'd dance better, should someone play...

FAUN
Who's got a flute or a recorder?
Pipe me a tune — but nothing sober!

OLD WOMAN
Where is Antek the herdboy?
C'mere! You got your little pipe?

(A little herdboy comes forth from the crowd — the people push him in the direction of the Faun — he pulls a little pipe out of his belt and begins to play, as he usually does when he's with his beasts)

OLD WOMAN
Come then sir, and choose a partner now.

HIRED HAND KUBA
And make it a pretty one!

FAUN
    (Approaches the crowd)
Who wants to dance with me?
You'll twirl with me
And then you'll skip
Like this —
    Hop, ha!
    (He takes one, she runs away; he takes another)

OLD WOMAN
Don't be skeered, Jaguś!
Not a leaf'll
Wither on your virgin wreath…
It's only a jig!

(One of the girls, more resolute, shyly approaches the Faun)

FAUN
Hurray!
Now, play!
  (He starts dancing, the herdboy plays)
Why so sadly?
Boldly! I want a tune to move my feet!

HIRED HAND KUBA
Play him to the beat
Like in the tavern-inn
Taram-lam-polka!
Or a waltz, so they can spin.
Or a štajer —

(The herdboy plays — the Faun dances — takes the girl around her waist, and they wheel about — the people start stamping their feet in time to the music)

FAUN
    (Sings)
The pipe is peeping, and I'm leaping, hu ha —
Although I'm old, I'm still a bold one, hu ha —
Like Bacchus dancing with his Flora, hu ha —
More lively than ever before-a, hu ha —
Earth and the gods laugh as they should now, hu ha —
    (Dancing ever more passionately, in a Terpsichorean frenzy, he lifts the girl into his arms and makes to run off into the forest with her)
And so we'll run off to the wood now, hu ha!
    (The girl screams)

HIRED HAND KUBA
    (Leaps and grabs him by a horn)
You faker you, I'll teach you a lesson!
It's girls you're after?
You dog-blooded bastard you...
(Beats him)

PEOPLE
    (Screaming)
— Give'm a wallop, the changeling!
— The son of a bitch, smash him!
— He drank the altar wine!
— Gets sloshed, an' he's after girls now, is he?
— Give'm one, right in the kisser!

(They all rush at the Faun, and beat him with hoes, staves, whatever they have to hand)

ORGANIST
    (Rushing up, terrified, trying to rescue the Faun, yelling)
People! Fear God!
What are you doing?

VILLAGE ALDERMAN
Stop it! Stop it!

PEOPLE
    (Beating the Faun, screaming)
— Here you go! Have some more!
— Whap him right between the horns!
— Knock them horns right off his head!
— We'll give'm horny, we will!
— Whap him! Wallop him!

(They literally fall upon him, trampling him)

OLD WOMAN
    (Rushing over)
Hey, people, hey!
The Reverend Father's on his way!

(Everyone runs off in fright — No one remains in the clearing but the bloodied, dying Faun)

FAUN
    (In an ever weaker voice)
And so I die —
Sun, and wood, goodbye;
Death is on her way for me
To take me, in this strange country.
The last Faun in the world
Killed by a peasant churl…
Forest, farewell.

Field, farewell.
Sun, farewell…
. . . .
I shall not see the corn to harvest swell,
Nor the culling of the vine,
It's time
For me to die.
Killed by a peasant churl,
A Barbarian…
(He dies)
— — — — — — — — —

(The Priest, Village Alderman, Organist, Lord and Lady of the Manor [She shaded by a parasol] enter the clearing)

ORGANIST
    (Narrating)
…And then they beat him
Sticks and hoes
Whatever there was to hand
And then they kicked him
Me and the alderman
We tried to rescue him…

VILLAGE ALDERMAN
We tried, Reverend Father
But what can you do when such a whole nation
Riles itself into a mob!
They were all set off, it seems,
When he grabbed a girl.

PRIEST
The boors, the churls!
To live amongst such rabble!
To live around here
Is to live in fear!
You can't let down your guard
For a moment's time.

As soon as I was out of sight
They took it in their heads to riot!

(The Lord and Lady of the Manor inspect the Faun)

LORD OF THE MANOR
Interesting.
Wonder how he came here.
And for one of our own peasants to kill him…
Well, one fairly blushes.
After all, he was a famous sort;
A guest from foreign parts.
We ought to let the papers know
How it was —
Not our fault, but that peasant's.
And after all our educational initiatives!
And you, alderman, where were you?

VILLAGE ALDERMAN
I beg your Grace,
We're innocent too! It's Kuba,
That hired hand…
So touchy about honour,
So hot-headed,
He started it all!

ORGANIST
Eh — If you please, your Grace…
He was — some sort of a… foreign god?

LORD OF THE MANOR
Well, there you have it:
A cultured sort.
Shouldn't have killed
A cultured sort.
And what does a peasant know
Other than whap and wallop?

LADY OF THE MANOR
    (Gazing at the Faun sprawled on the ground)
Eh — he was already an old fellow.
He didn't need much any more.
Come on — it's so nasty, near a corpse.
It's hot, too. Soon he'll start
To smell. Let's go.

LORD OF THE MANOR
We've got to send someone
To carry him away.
— — — Well, and so dies
The last of his kind,
The last Faun,
And on Polish soil!

(They go off)

(A Girl comes out into the clearing — stands near the corpse of the Faun — gazes at him)

GIRL
Eh — he's dead. — They kilt him.
And here it's springtime,
So pretty…
The sun so strong and warm…
Eh, little sun!

(Distant song from the wood)

SONG
Hey recruit, my sweet recruit,
Take that spur from off your boot —
It may be good for coaxing mares,
But I demand some gentler care.
      Hu — ha — a

GIRL
       (Responds in song as loudly as she can)
In the spring, the sweet springtime,
The warm sun is on the climb.
Now the winter's over
Come to me, my lover,
Jaś, you sweetheart of mine!
       Hu — ha — a

(The refrain dies away in the woods — silence ensues. The sun is at its highest point. Church bells from the village ring for midday — It's hot and humid — from the woods can be heard the thumping of cattle)

GIRL
    (Calls)
Antoska — they're ringing the Angelus.
Drive in the herd — they're getting restless!...

THE END

The Green Eye. Formistic Poems. Electric Visions

(1907)

The Green Eye

The Tiger's Eyes

Black vertical lines
Yellow greenery the sea
      The hum of violet
Chee chee
The cry of a monkey
Blue stripes of greenery
Azure yellow violet palms a cloud
The cry of a bird of purple
    hee hee
On his livid paw he treads
      Silently
The gigantic green **eye**
The other eye bloodily green
Monkeys chee chee
Parrots hee hee
    The green eye
A greenish-white mass
Violet in the ring
The simian heart trembles
Pulsing mysterious blood
    The green eye
The palms rustle the Rhododendron waits
    Butterflies flit
The eye keeps watch unmoving

Purply-verdant
        And the **other**
        Green **eye**
Terror drowses
Monkeys shee-shee
Parrots hee-hee
        Green eyes
Is it night already   is it day already
        Is it a dream
Is it fear — is it hypnotism
Palms   Silence   Dusk
Monkeys   Butterflies   Parrots
Chee-chee hee-hee chee-chee
        THE GREEN EYE.

Halfsleep

(in a fever)

there stands my soldier's bed
on the bed I neither sleep nor watch
half-whispered rustles of prayer
fear with the face of a ghoul before sleep
this is my soldier's bed
booted feet tread
over my stomach and chest
I hear the moan of the dying
people approach with weapons
a dog vomiting bullets
and cold fingers on my eyes
the fingers of **nemesis-death**
the sun peeped out of white clouds
I felt a palm upon my face
soft snowy bell like a lily's
and white as her bosom's bouquet
the herbs are fragrant the forest sighs
where am I where am I ah where
does **He** cry does **She**

I adore you my brother sleep
then a dull cry resounded
my beloved voice took flight
platoon attention shoulder arms
rat tat a tat the gun I sleep.

Dread

a knife on a naked throat and blood
thousands of banknotes of green
ooo howls the dog in pain *ooo*
        hand it over or you're dead

night after night an escape into fear
the humid torment of incarceration
aaa ecstasy laps up the blood
        hand it over or you're dead

I am the master a kaftan of red
hand over hand over the blood
thousands of banknotes of grey
        hand it over or you're dead

four soldiers stand with their backs to the wall
a blindfold of white over the eyes
a cold bullet a bloodied brain
        hand it over or you're dead

Music from a Window
Sob

        for Zofia Ordyńska

and so it occurred on one autumn **night**
right at my feet there fell a withered **flower**

above me a balcony empty and dark
above the balcony a ringing **song**
and thus it occurred on one autumn **night**
when I was buffeted by sadness and **wind**
beneath a dark and empty balcony
music laughed out from the window, and **light**
and thus it so happened on one autumn **night**
while was passing beneath the balcony
right at my feet there fell a withered **flower**
from the dark window there flew out no **laughter**
once it so happened on one autumn **night**
through the dark window one could hear **sobs**.

Dance

for Jan Hryńkowski

Laughter — sound…
           rings…
Stomping — light —
           Candelabras. —

Sound — shiver…
           ha,
Frock, red, green,
           frenzy!…
Key: — C, A

***

Ecstasy — frenzy
A naked breast revealed
A golden frock, violet — white —
Strikes against bronze.
Wheels — fiery — rainbows
        a Flash.

***

The line of an arch… a back —
      Silence!
Moan, pain and frenzy,
        Purple
The flash grows dark,
The grey twilight flies.

FEAR

In a dark and mealy-rotten wood
Dusk falls on the thick limbs of trees
(Fear takes possession of my mind)
The shadow falls on yellow leaves
The shadow falls on rusty moss
(Through the sky there are birds that fly)
(From the limbs there are leaves that fly)
There is a black pool in the ancient wood
The wind swept through the fields of wheat
Swept through the silent fields at noon
(And there still dances the bloody noon-witch)
              ha – ha
          The Wind
Struck in the mountain vales
Struck like a sublunar wave
(Owl badger bat are all asleep)
              Mysteries
Firstly green rings of ripples roll about the water
A leaf of burdock leans aside
A water lily begins to glow with its pale light
Yellow bubbles roll about the water
Swarms of flashing beetles are awing
              Silence
A bloodcurdling scream
Naiads goddesses rusalkas mamunas
I want to be ravished in ecstasy I want

***

The vesper bell has rung
The blackbird has whistled
Falling asleep
Ave Maria – Ave Maria

***

In the depths of the pool I see eyes
Staring eyes
I see my terrified
                    Eyes

CITY. AUTUMN EVENING
(ANTI-IDYLL)

warm astrakhans — here, put 'em on
it's way past zero centigrade
from the café a drunken song
booms a dissonant serenade
there in the church they're ringing bells
someone gives someone a swift boot
on the canal mist swirls and swells
the howling dogs have all gone mute
the smiling sun now glumly goes
as smoke slides over the rooftop
while now and then a rooster crows
and from the graveyard rhymes drip-drop
the whore's car speeds off to the night
the tram sweeps off down the wide street
cheeks with céruse are powdered white
slippers are on the corpse's feet
I smell the fresh scent of wet clay
they beat the rugs on clothespoles hung
mi fa so la si do re
there's ladders rung after white rung

in nurseries the babes are crying
while clouds float slowly through the air
the purples of the dawn are shining
through the tatters of human despair

City

Thrown across the misty Seine those
Bridges like rusty clamps bind tight
The city near the green stream two rows
Of houses that passed a sleepless night
Blink tired windows
                         people vans
Jam bridge and street a roiling wedge
And there a snarled string of trams
All of this sets my nerves on edge
Everyone rushes to the streets
Everyone buys or hustles sells
And thus the city's pulse beats beats
Along the street man's thought seeps swells
That crowd of people cars and cheats
Some unknown common end foretells

Rebellion

Through ages that like minutes
            flow
Underground work in secret
            goes on
And sometimes the underground
        pit gives birth to earthly
            acts.

The underground worker takes
            earthly shape
So that some unearthly thought

              or act
Become flesh to terrify
              you man
And then the secret labour
              resumes
It's weapons they're fashioning
              and bombs
Stacking those weapons as if
              in arsenals awaiting
              the day
On which begins the battle
(to steal the sun from him
              and rule the world)

They'll declare war on
              the Pre-eternal
The ages fly and man's thoughts
              incandesce
The work goes on in secret
              forges
And people start to despise
              divine protection
(And God summons His prophets
              Isaiah Nathaniel
              David)

The work goes on in the dark
              depths

Fool's Monologue

The bells from the rose-coloured church
Sing out over the entire quarter
Beyond the city on a hill grow
Bushes of wild hawthorn, may trees
The bells of the church nearby
Toll for the matins of the dead

Beneath a hawthorn bush a rotting
Face rests in the earth
Did you see the flowing blood
Did you see the fool's eyes
A look of despair and of dreaming
The eternal shank of evening
The despair of one man
The sadness and laughter of a town entire
The speckled giggle of the fool
I am he who rose from the bed
     at the green hour
     of the frantic *sun*
I am he who rinsed his eyes
In the flooding mountain stream
Swiftly bearing floes of ice
     cracked and melting
I am he whose motley tongue
Touches people's heads
I am he whose frigid hands
Lay upon beating hearts
I play upon men some notes
In the key of despair
I play upon men a song
Which is the song of sweetness
But the moment of silence approaches
When I invite *death*
I rack the hearts on the green felt
And hand the cue to death *you break*

Summer Evening

All over the village one hears the dogs howl
Some herd boy sadly blows his flageolet
In the old linden, mournfully hoots an owl
Among the alder leaves a bat swoops and swirls
Giggling their way back from the field come the girls
And gloomy night rings down the toilsome day

The last glow of the crimson twilight fails
As from caves, clouds crawl down mountain tops
Black monsters drag along repulsive tails
They drag near cloudy night full of unease
While marsh frogs play their yearning symphonies
And here and there drowses the lonely copse

Between the houses as the dark evening falls
On the orchard where lindens and pear-trees stand
Something, a secret shadow, coddiwomples, crawls
And on the rough-hewn door lays withered hand
His sad face floats up to the bright window

Inside, a peasant sharpens scythe toward tomorrow

A blacksmith's hammer rings out from the forge
A conversation loud and violent
The blacksmith's hammering shoes for a horse
The iron takes shape, the sparks fly, brightly glowing
Such a song from the struck anvil is sent
Men repair blades toward tomorrow's mowing
Along the road the spectre crawls and winds
Clutching the roadside trees with withered hands
Searching the gloom with sunless rotten eyes
Scraping along, furrowing the grey sands.

CATHEDRAL

The Gothic pillars soar up to the vault
Where into dry stone branches see them grown
Here in the church cool silent shadows drowse
Nothing here but dark blue boulders, stone
Then through the panes the flames of sunlight crash
Curtains of amaranth reflect the flash
And dull stained glass now glows and burns bright hues
Of yellows violets greens and crimsons
So deep the church that thought errs lost inside

Its strictly measured stiffnesses of stones
Where like a coiling snake the echoes glide

So flames the silence in the human brain
God and His temple seem to constitute
An ideal mysterious and unattained

THE SLEEP OF FLOWERS

Amongst the flowers exhausted with desires
Glides **Sleep** *pale lilies of the valley drowse*
The slender figure of narcissus bows
Sweetly caressed the pansies close their eyes

Amongst the flowers exhausted with desires
Glides memory following in her train
Comes her companion: winged pain
Sets the soul where night's gloomy grotto lies

The night emerges and with its black wing
Covers the garden flowers and the plain
Into the other world she the soul conveys

While sleeps the earth the flowers and everything
Above the earth die off the last red rays
And nothing wakes but memory winged pain

A POEM OF NUMBERS

      0   1
Instruments of Unity
      2   4
Raucous and great
That dance
      6   8
The family 141

Going out for a stroll
The company of humble numbers
    1   5   11
Stupid numbers
    24   25
Shameless numbers
    41   42
Unlucky numbers
    3   13   33
Ill-boding numbers
Like the odd numbers of houses
Like seven cows gaunt and
    Biblical
Week   Month   Year
7   30   365
The grand harmony of numbers and stars
The harmony of the waking soul
    9   7   9
The Harmony of Circle Triangle Square
    Enduring Motion
        Eternity

SINGING HOUSES

The houses stroll the street
    Singing
The green house
    Sad
Along another street stroll
Singing houses
    Gay ones
  The white house
    Sings baritone
The slender yellow house
    Soprano
      Each is different
They rush and glance

    The windowpanes crash to the cobbles
        Shining and tinkling
            I passed them
From afar hearing the singing
            Houses
The red   The white   The yellow
        House

RAIN

The rain rings on the balcony of stone
The windblown chestnuts sigh before the house
While past the very horizon speed on the clouds
Their lightning bolts like gold on an icon
The saddened roses in the gardens swoon
The lightnings' afterglow fills them with dread
They've tightly furled their petals crimson-red
Their cruses pummelled to one weeping wound
Why has this sadness overcome the trees
Why has this sadness overcome the blooms
The heart is searching for scabbed-over wounds
The wind hums on its ghoulish melodies
Uncomforted by their unceasing mourning
Can sunlight revive these flowers in the morning.

BELL

The bell on the tower
                      Rings
                Resurrecturi
            The sun spurts light
          Diamonds streetpuddles
The thunderous bell
                      Rings
              Resurrecturi
             The singing bell

                    Rings
                  Resurrection
      The procession winds around the church
                  They carry the naked Christ
                      With the red banner
              Christ has risen from the dead
                      Resurrecturi
                  The bell on the tower
                          Rings
      The odour of ploughed fields on the breeze
                      The fleecy new green
              And thou shalt resurrect O earth
                      to thee they sing
                      Resurrecturi
                      for thee the bell
                          RINGS.

Moment of Sadness

Why have you come here
Moment of sadness!
The heavens neither weep
Nor behind black clouds do they creep
The trees neither moan
Nor does the earth churn with groans
No mournful owl hoots
No bitterness takes root
In my heart Where
Do you come from Afar
From where no man's soul plumbs the mystery
From a land of cursed eternity
Where aeons ago by God
    Begotten you were
    Moment of sadness!

ODE TO BREAD

O grain conceived within the sunny field
Who from the fecund Polish soil was grown
Who into strong black flour one day was milled
And from that flour became this loaf of brown
Today in praise of thee I tune my lute
Bread, as I place thy loaf upon the table
Gazing at thee in sadness thus I brood…
Upon the sorrows of this teary vale…
. . . .
O bread black bread bread born of toil and strain
Today it is for thee I make this paean.
. . . .
When Sacred Host in gold cyborium
The heart of the blest elements I admire
In cryptic gloom of oratorium
Attended by the archangelic choir
O bread black bread bread born of toil and strain
Today it is for thee I make this paean.
. . . .
When on a shaky table round which stand
A group of children pale and underfed
Each stretching toward the fresh round loaf a hand —
While their mother slices thin the strong black bread
In the dank crowded tenement basement
Her mind drifts off to those not present…
One girl sits at a cinema register
Another rolls cigars throughout the day
A third's out hawking the Evening Courier
A fourth one walks the streets to earn her pay…
. . . .
O bread black bread bread born of toil and strain
Today it is for thee I make this paean!
. . . .
And there in the 'Concertinocafé'
Where soothed by song a man might meditate
And sometimes dream the while the fiddles play
Or sigh or yawn (as long as one's discreet)

At a round table like King Arthur's knights
Should one feel peckish as one sips one's beer
There's nothing wrong with calling for a bite
'Hey waiter! More bread and butter over here!'…
. . . .
O bread black bread bread born of toil and strain
Today it is for thee I make this paean!

Melody of the Crowd

The river of the boulevard
    That swells before my eyes
A procession of skeletons
        Above the barber's
    shop
The wind sets fluttering
        the tin disc

Pimps   maidens
        Streetgutter ragamuffins
Tramway   omnibus   auto
And all the horns are blaring
    ha   ha
In the bar they've eaten sandwiches
    Drunk coffee and whisky
More plates are brought up briskly

The river of the boulevard
        In the café
    A green flute
    A woman's breast
    Attention
        Castanets
Red rings shivers
Someone gets
    aroused
        Nervous lights

        In brackets
Eyes   Hands Thoughts
  without faces
      frigid corridors
        A p p l a u d i n g w i n d o w s
          Telephone
     A lift swift and loud
 unease   dread
     Searching for *someone*
    IN THE CROWD

Silence

Through a gloomy chamber
  tread quiet feet unshod
      whisper thoughts unspoken
        secreted sadness
        uncomplaining impotence
        someone's jostled the strings
        of the harp on the wall
        someone's lips are quivering
at the most beautiful moment
        neither weeps
       nor cheeps
      my sleeping vulture

quiet thoughts go out in the world
  float on currents of air
    peer into hearts
      are astonished
      forgive
        awaken and remember
       converse
     go along a thousand wires
    a thousand cables
      out into the world

in the gloomy chamber, silence

PERCEPTION

To Leon Chwistek

In the knarriest matter
   The dark spirals of the snail
      Everything can be fathomed
      and associated

Like rains that flow
Like clouds that blow
Thoughts flash and go
Vain words of note
Like rains that flow
Like death that is no more

The snail that pauses
on a humble blade of grass
To consider nature from above
Gazes at cities villages vales
     understands the totality of things
The mystery of the rolling wheel
Number   Nature   Death
    ?
   Like
   Man

When he rocks in the boat
  he sailed out on at dawn
    certainly foreseeing
    while seeing n o t h i n g

>   to come at last into a foreign port
>   where perception is
>   **Never** or **Nothing**

For Art and Life

> For M. Jan Bołoz-Antoniewicz

For the construction of worlds start
With FORM *the style of bloom and art*
The hammer strikes the house is made
The quartz is sawn by the mason's blade
A life over-gigantic flies
An ocean of fire high in the skies
The spreading of Magnolia flowers
Beneath the Will's and Reason's powers
The day re-azures as dawn breaks
A wave of spiral tremblings quake
The atoms' nervous jerky throes
The steep planetary roads
Crackling radioactive currents
Misty fires that sputter and dance
The rhythmics that hands clutch and grip
Embarking on a cosmic trip
From art through STYLE to what abides
The spirit to harmony inclines
Where senseless form will have no part
Where now is birthing the new art.

Erotica

A Glimpsed Face

Across the way — the silver-grey pane
    Of the café —
    One, two, three,
    Across the way
'Coffee,'   **'Mazagran'**   **'Grenadine.'**
A white hand holds
    A newspaper.
Four, five, six —
    Across the way
I see half the face
    Of a woman. —
Mud spurts from beneath a tyre,
    The heart pounds.
Across the way
    It's her
Reading the 'Journal des débats.'
She looks down: seven, eight,
I see **two and a half faces!**
    No!
It's not her — eh — bah!!
It was a phantom…
She turns her eyes upon me,
No — it's not her,
I see white teeth —
    — The brain grows dim —
A smile and a gold filling,
It's not her.

Le soir d'amour

'Close the window'…
'The moon's come into the room,'
    'It'll smash the lamp,'

　　　　'Close the window,'
　　　　'The wind,'
　　　　'The moon.'
'Fell into the water basin.'
　　　'Let me go,'
　　　　'Don't kiss me,'
'The moon, Close the Window, The wind.'
　　　　Watch out.
Her slipper's come undone
'Close the window.'
　　　　The moon,
　　　　　　The wind!!

Alleycat Serenade

Oa   oa   oa

That cat's in need of love and how
Here in my room I sit and hear
Curled near my lamp in the quiet
His drawn out lubricious meow

　　au　　　au　　　o - a - u

Grey roof, the rising moon's advance
Here a quadrille there champagne flutes
The hotel does a can-can dance

Mrau   au - u

A slut is chased by sharps in suits
The streets leap everything flies
The phosphorous flash of cats' eyes
The cat is sick with love, the miss
Is ailing herself: chlorosis
He's lost his soul — that cat's a wreck

I lie here in my lonely room
I hear the tomcat wail and scream
My nerves — I'll wring my own damn neck

Mrau   au   au
The bottles squeak in the buffet
Drin   drin   drin

The naughty kitchen help at play
hee   hee   hee u ee   hee
I listen and I cannot sleep
A car screws through street after street
The shine of gaslamps
Up on the roof he wails and weeps
He curls his tail and then he leaps
From chimney to floor to cornice
'Tis he, the artist of the roofs
The lord of chimneys tomcat **mrau**
I try to think I try to read
Lives of the saints Hoesick Boy
Then somebody behind the wall
Cries out in love's ecstasy **Oy**
It's midnight all the steeples ring
bom   bum   bum   bom
Mrau mrau longing **mrau**
I leap from bed in a wild trance
I cannot sleep I'm shivering
I nervously pull on my pants
Love — so I rush out in the street
To look for love adventure calls
I'll scrape my flank against the walls
Tomcat I'm searching for a kitten
Soon down a dark lane see me flittin'
Somebody's twanging a guitar
I ring the doorbell, wait, and then
This busty slag opens hawking phlegm
Behind my back I hear **mrau u**

Remembering the Mountains

Mountains Valleys and Rivers
    Conversed with one another
The moon rose and lost its way
    along a road of many smiles
    A wayside bird plummeted
        in the mist
    Today I have a rendez-vous
    With Her the laughing girl
        The light
    reflected from the stream
Shining like the Books the words
        that shimmer in my thought
    In which I chanced upon
        a dry pressed rose
Moon   Love
Mountains   Valleys   Rivers
    Sadness   *Gladness*
    The Way.

Betrayal

She went she felt she was with child
She lay down on a sidewalk bench
He grabbed his browning and he bit
You bitch this is betrayal bitch

Who took the wallet from the sideboard
Who was it sang to the police
She fell like a bitch in the street
This is the blood of life and crime

The telephone screams and the crowd
Says that the girl is innocent
She shudders on the hospital bed
And there's a child and blood and shit

He sleeps at home all liquored up
His moll in hospital like a dog
Say that I kilt 'im kilt 'im dead
No need for death now no need now

The child of a father unknown
You knew you knew that it was me
They came you knew and with handcuffs
You knew you bitch that it was ME.

Electric Visions

> *O Christ I wish to glimpse*
> *the shadow of the shadow of Thy*
> *fire of Delight*

Introduction

The guest of orange cynicism

Near my spring-heeled *House*
   In the dark night there draws near
      A Rooster who crows and calls
         Clock
I hear him he goes past the door
        the wary dog barks
Somebody knocks I hear a yellow voice
      Open up
Would you like to go to the land of the
      black aurora
Of the red skull of the grave of graves
    I
Am the one you got to know
As a child
I like to play on a grand keyboard
     I dance
In the sacristy the dance of the skeletons
You know me from the village church
      That burnt down
As your *Thoughts* were burnt to the ground
     By the fires of gall and cynicism
I am the one of whom you thought
     Not thinking
    Man
   you seek a dam
  In the squinted winter Night
You bribed your Fate   you avoid *death*
   Who drinks in the dive

'At the Platinum Scales'
Take up the staff garlanded with ivy
Girdle your hips and be off.

Vision I

                      The talons of the fear of man
                      The joy of revelation
                      PAIN rocks the cradle of the child

    I ⟶   In the Name of the *Motor* Ghost
                            Amen
I go I see *I* and my guest
The earth drags on white bearing
        A Roadside *Cross*
    Millions and millions of miles
Bells of crystal
Frozen   Rivers
Skeleton   and   *Puss*
millions and millions of miles
Slavery   **Despair**   **Night**   *Aurora*
   millions and millions of miles
Sky   burning   Suns
   millions and millions of
       Miles
Green   blue   yellow
   millions and millions of
       Miles
Legs have become bowed from dancing the stomach quivers
People   Animals   Lizards
The coffins of ideals dance
Millions and millions of miles
ho   ho   ha
The Dance of cynicism the Dance
    of cogs and wheels.
    Fire   Earth   Water

    Diamonds chrysoprase   sapphires of
               Redes      INRI

They hung a sign on look

On the hill beweeping the city
The Cross that jibbers
The tin sign chatters
          Drinking gall

     O   U   O
Three times speeds the lightning bolt
The revelation the mechanical wonder
The grave built of diamonds
The motor spinners and the brain
The cradle with the puling child
        The breaking sun and the pain
Machine   Eagle   Earth
Ganymede
and his Lord   *Dynamo*

            Pam Bam
    Fire   *Earth Water*

INTERMEZZO

FLOWERS OF PREY

Poppies drunk on blood
It was it was in the depths
Irony was the feeling the dream of the sheep
A cup of unleavened honey
Yellow bees the mother
The linden rustling with the swarm
The shattered tree

The smoking embers of the house
The scurvy corpse of the cat
Maggots and worms at the dried up cloaca
~~~~~~~~~~~~~~~~~~~~~~~~~~~~~~
My synthesis draws near

And now I'm off to the sensorial
To the omnipotent Machine of
      My Reason

Vision II

              I delight in the fact
              that I shall survive myself

To enter the blue day

The night is passed, day after day here
      The brindled carrotty panther draws near
Two shining arrows his electric eyes
His brain acres-broad like a metro
Black eyes each a pulsing dynamo
      Two wheels burning without fires

    Oa   *Oa*   *Oa*
    R   R   R

I stretch my naked arms out before me
My two arms like soaring avianwings
I see mountains rivers polyps tentacles
I touch the forests hills valleys
I seek baptism orders liberties
I see my friends gathered at a masked ball
    At the king's in the Escorial
Columbina Polichinelle Titania
the Dream and the Ass's Head
    the Beast discolourèd

Through the window of the spice shop
I see the loavers of bread kissing
The world's comedy lottery numbers
Work-worn shivering cities
The swollen graveolent land
      The rivers intermingle
      The oceans all unite
    Winds Clouds
    From a corpse's skull
        grows a
      Sheaf
The clowns laughed out by the light of lightbulbs
        Fashion plates in stripes
Earth's actions dancers of yellow pom-poms
        Bordello porters
The locksmiths of human consciences
      the Sheaf bleeds
      the gore of the soil
      God blesses the

      Sheaf

VISION III

The electric dawn

THE MECHANICS OF MIRACLE
THE ART OF GREEN TEETH

pam – bam mighty God

    I
We stood above a one-eyed livid lake
The fires of all the chimneys
The fires of all the furnaces of crystal

THAT OTHER ONE

The lake   the dawn breaks   the winds
Over the lake a hail of diamonds
The tensity could not have been more fierce
In the lake the golden shadow disappears
Du-ada-du-ada-ada-dill
The herdsman toots the cattle down the hill

THE POET

It's time to fly away the day is here
Ouzel thrushes eagle wolf
Duada-duada-ada-dill
They toot the hymn on wooded hills

THE HERDSMAN *afar*

Duada-dadu-udu-du

THAT OTHER ONE

Smoking chimneys flames toxic gas
The traces of materials that relax
Matter in which steel, iron took such delight
Urano-flashes of nebulous white
Mechanics Spirit wam boo
    Verily I say unto you
(afar one can hear the death-song)

THAT SAMEOTHER ONE

Can you hear the dream-song

THE POET

I can hear a sprouting song
(afar one can hear a toothèd moan)
ty r r r – hr r r

THAT SAMEOTHER ONE

A new art and a column new
Minerva's owl prophet hoo-hoo
Boom boom they're building a home
Bam bam whams the hammer
Spring spring bursts forth a spring
Fear fear is passed no fear
I strum my lute to the ages
Allei – alleluia to us

I

BE BORN:

A lily flavour a sudden black flare
From the lake a great bird takes to the air
The Poet and *Sameother One* have disappeared
The factories collapse the chimneys flash
Above the lake rose the electric Dog
The mighty God of future humanity
Quiet helpless strongman and lord
        Spirit

Ah – pam – bam

No end but beginning

When delight has been appeased
When the bricks unite in love

When the soil dissolves in ochre day
When the silence weeps in baby piss
When the sarcophagi are scabbed over
Then I shall arise
Then the begotten sun
Then the incandescent maid
And the electric husband Oo
Hosanna Hosanna to You.

(1919)

The Snake, Orpheus and Eurydice

A Classical Vision

(1922)

'Dynamopsycho'

within each of my drawings, from 1 – 15, are found dynamo psychic stadia, which occur at certain moments. Each of these pictures is my DYNAMOPSYCHO

Tytus Czyżewski
Kraków, 25/V. 1922

As
over mountains and hills the sun goes
down, clouds, cranes, the moon grows
above the lake above its depths
Orpheus converses with his lyre.

ORPHEUS
              (with his lyre)
The strings of my lyre are gold
snakes of blue heaven and gold
eyes made of diamonds and teeth
reflect the glare back to the sun
waves metamorphosed to clouds
clouds transformed into quadrigas
birds and fish.

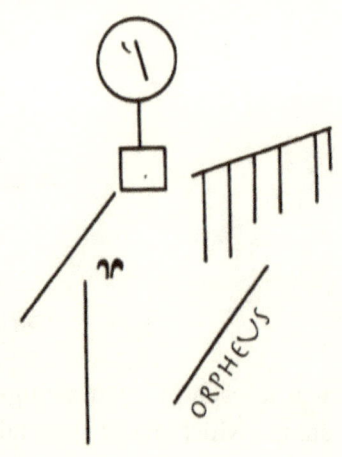

EURYDICE
              (emerges from the grotto)
persephone persephone
dandles puppies on her knee.

ORPHEUS
              (to Eurydice)
Eurydice wait my dear
the man from the cinema's here
over the fields the frogs trill
there's blooming lilies, a rill.

EURYDICE
I've had enough of hell
and the untanned halftones
of telephones and microphones.

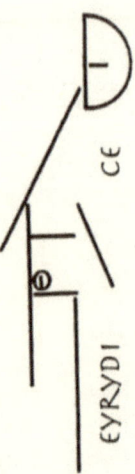

ORPHEUS
             (approaching the grotto)
close the ventilators
hired hands of manly Pluto
that's enough fresh air for now
             (the huge gates of the grotto close,

ORPHEUS
             (twangs his lyre)

EURYDICE
             (begins to twirl slowly on her axis

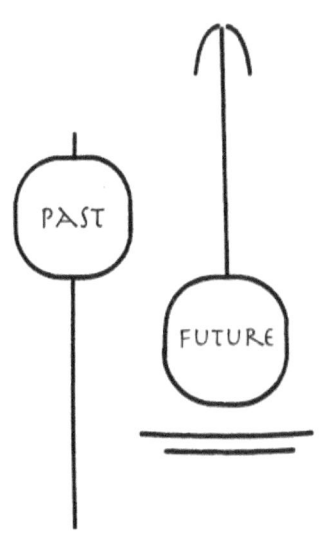

ORPHEUS
the conjurer chisels in marble
the divine thighs of aphrodite

Burning with passion
I beg Eurydice in vain
sending my telegraphic signals
from station to station
you Eurydice are not listening
you Eurydice do not love me.

EURYDICE
in vain in the underworld perishing
I was tormented with sad thoughts
why are you weeping Orpheus.

ORPHEUS
they're snapped — the strings of my lyre
and my fingers with effort expire
songs and scherzos and études
no longer make my heart to ooze.

A BURGLAR OF THE BETTER SORT

EURYDICE
              (sadly)
so you no longer rave on my account.

ORPHEUS
I've purchased two gramophones
that play along with my lyre.

EURYDICE
you mock your lyre.

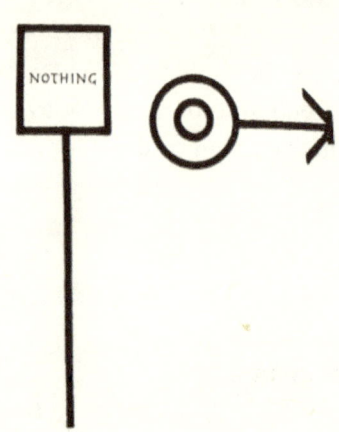

ORPHEUS
neither forest nor mountain existed then
only frenzied frothing rivulets
when I learned how to compose songs.

EURYDICE
back then I was weaving the linen white
of my shirt at my mother's side
and my breasts burst into bloom.

ORPHEUS
your flowers have all come into bloom
give yourself to me Eurydice.

TYTUS CZYŻEWSKI

EURYDICE
and your lyre what will your lyre do.

(Eurydice and Orpheus approach one another)
*(Eurydice unbuttons the robe on her bosom
and uncovers her white breasts)*

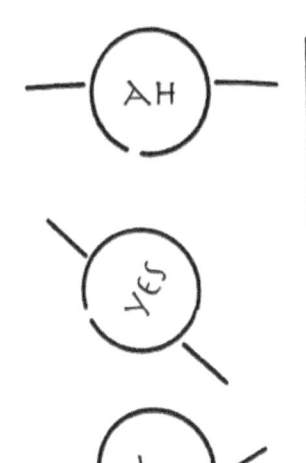

ORPHEUS
— throws his lyre upon the ground —
— the lyre — shatters —
— a factory siren is heard in the distance —
— the sun has set — from beyond the lake

a gigantic moon slowly rises
and is reflected upon the water.

orpheus and eurydice
are now joined in an embrace
they stand motionless
one hears a distant singing
a group of young boys is singing and dancing
(on staves they carry baskets full of grapes)

they sing and they play
bacchus bacchus
you limp asparagus
what have you done you clown,
spilling your seed on the ground.

You silly jackanapes
sowing for pumpkins and grapes
while orchard and rose are red
and we've wreaths upon the head.

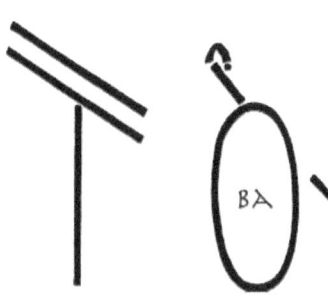

A BURGLAR OF THE BETTER SORT

In the olive grove nearby
there's sweet smelling moss and grass,
how sweet it is, old boy, to lie
there, couched upon a naked lass.
    (they pass by and grow silent)

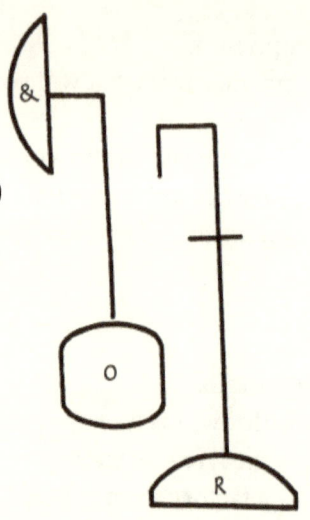

 ORPHEUS AND EURYDICE
united in an embrace
in the light of the moon

grow completely pale
and become a marble statue
slowly ivy over creeps them
the moon sails the heavens
the field crickets chirp
one hears the startling whistle
of a steam locomotive
    (silence)

the gates of the grotto open slowly
**from within one hears the bell
of a telephone ringing**
    which
   (grows silent)
from the grotto there crawls
a gigantic **PYTHON SNAKE**
it nears
the statue of Eurydice and Orpheus
winds itself around them in an embrace
the statue totters and falls into the lake

 . . . .

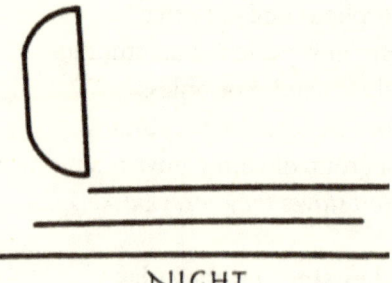

NIGHT

an **EPHEBUS** arrives

playing a small lute and singing:

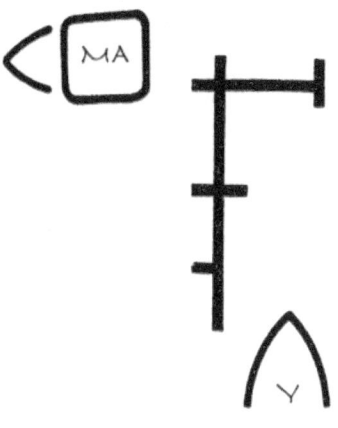

when I was a little boy
I sucked at my ma's firm breasts
I knew I would become a man
someday, a man, a grownup man
a man impregnating women

blackhaired lovers and redheads
or those with curly golden hair
                (he passes on)
. . . .

from afar a procession nears singing
carrying on a dhooly
a gigantic **Phallus**

          (they sing)
     Phallus, Phallus, Phallus
     you impregnate our mothers
     our sisters our daughters
     our wives and our lovers
     O Phallus, O Phallus.

Because of you Phallus
the water, the earth live
Because of you Phallus
the gods and mankind exist
O Phallus, O Phallus.

*(they set the sculpture on the ground
they kneel and bow before it)*

a cloud covers the moon
it grows dark
a red light erupts
from the prostrate **Phallus**,
which is transformed into
a gigantic **electric lightbulb**.

. . . .

The gates of the grotto open
revealing the naked god of the underworld
Pluto, covered in coal dust
hammer slung over his shoulder, he shouts:

    DYNAMOPHALLUS!!
suddenly, everyone disappears — there remains
the **phallus lightbulb** glowing red.

DYNAMOPHALLUS

Donkey and Sun in Metamorphosis

(1922)

To my Friends and my Opponents

This play was produced on 28 November and 4 December 1921 at the literary courses in Kraków, under the direction of Prof. Marian Szyjkowski, with the actors of the Bagatela Theatre:

FROG...Mme Trojanowska
DONKEY..M Heniowski
SUN..M Broński
FIELD HAND / HAYCOCK......................M Łukasiewicz
FLY...Mlle Kowalikówna
FUTURIST..........................M Stanisław Młodożeniec (the poet)

The scenario was read by M. Leszko
Costumes created and decorations painted by Waliszewski, Jarema and Czyżewski.

Persons:

SUN: A rotund personage, bright, with long rays. A 'nightcap' is stuck on the end of one of his rays. On the sun's face — a clock showing 11:30.
FROG: An old coquette, in green stripes and pink hat.
DONKEY: An intelligent intellectual ass.
FIELDHAND: A vulgar type.
HAYCOCK: No different from the Fieldhand.
FLY: Buzzing.

The action takes place in a four-dimensional universe.

Donkey and Sun in Metamorphosis
A formo-satirico-bouffonade

      Persons, animals and planets
      A flying thing: an aeroplane
Immoral surroundings
Trees horizontal and at rakish angles
Sky to the front of the stage
Disorder and illogicity onstage
      The audience ought to imagine that there is a pond in the depths of the stage

> **For morality's sake bathing here is permitted only to those wearing masks.**

At the centre of the stage there is a sign, on which is writ in red letters:At the pond's edge sits a frog, fishing with a pole.
Green colour dominates the stage.
Next to the pond, a gramophone is playing.
The gramophone runs down. After a momentary pause, a distant chorus of frogs is heard:

      Ragi nagi,   ragi nagi
      eh   eh   eh
      he croaked the stork he croaked
      Ragi nagi

FROG

    (fishing)

      uag uag
      Ragi nagi

(the green light on stage grows ever stronger)

FROG
Take my hook fish take my hook
waook — waook — waook

The stage brightens.
From behind the stage the sleepy
          old sun enters, carrying a parasol.
The sun walks over the stage witth an unsteady gait.

SUN

    (yawning)
Ua – ha
What an excruciating bore.
I'll take a little walk and go back indoors.
    (looks about the sky)
And not a bloody cloud from here to doom
To hide behind — what a day. Such gloom.
Br……rr
    (suddenly catching sight of the frog)
What's this? A frog with a fishing cane?
And kind of a — kind of a dame —
Well, that's some phenomenon!!

FROG

    (turning to the sun that is crossing the stage slowly, reeling somewhat)
Well, there's a marvellous omen on
A fine day! The sun in a good humour!
Darling sun — 'Bon jour,'
You electro-lamp of the day,
Earth's magisterial gas-inspector.
How come so late in dawning?

SUN

    (stretching and yawning)
Ua…
I slept in a bit this morning.
I didn't get to bed too soon
Last night — had a confab with the moon
About the plunging interest rates,
About the price of leather skates.
    (yawns)

Uhaa – a.
We played a few hands
Of whist, drank a bit and… romanced
A tad…
And the old head is pounding. Bad.
> *(The sun continues across the stage, shambling)*

FROG
> *(with irony)*

What's nature coming to, damn her,
If even the sun wakes with a katzenjammer!

SUN
Ha… O well, my dear lady,
It's tough to watch the livelong day
Idiots and jackasses at their capers,
Devising new wars…
The times are getting worse.
. . . .
Our deliberations have started none too soon,
Mine and the moon's,
. . . .
Of course,
You'll read what we've come up with in the papers…

FROG
> *(intrigued)*

You'll be printing the entire manifesto?

SUN
Yes — yes — yes — yes…
And reading it aloud in the star chamber, then, presto!
Oh, intellectual labour is so tiring!
> *(The sun takes its head in its hands)*

FROG
As for me, curiosity keeps me fired
Up, sleepless all night long, up-stirred
With restless thoughts...

SUN
            ... And thoughts absurd
Fill my poor nut as well...

FROG
At night my frog-legs ache like hell.
O yo-yo-yo-yoy!

SUN
I'm so worn out at day's end.

FROG
            One thing's clear,
Old sun, we're both getting on in years!

SUN
For such old rags, patch as patch can, my dear.

(Suddenly, the distant, muffled braying of a donkey)
(The donkey — a very elegant one — enters. He has a 'bowler' on his head, a belted coat, a monocle in one eye, and a bunch of newspapers pressed between foreleg and chest)

DONKEY
    (braying)
Ua — uaa... a...
How prettily the sun is shining!
I can smell the blooming clover.
Makes the mouth water! I'll just amble over
For a bit of browsing, dining,
u ha ha

FROG
> *(to herself)*

Ooh such manners ooh such grace,
And what a handsome donkey face!

DONKEY
> *(to himself)*

Well, how's that for a sweet amphibian girl?
I wouldn't mind giving that frog a whirl…

FROG
> *(to herself)*

This can be no coincidence!
This donkey, famous and so grand,
Born of passion asinine,
An artist to his marrowed bones,
An arbiter of liberal arts?

DONKEY
> *(to himself)*

This can be no coincidence!
That famous rurico-idyllic
Idy-lyri-irical batrachian
Erato-classico-epical
Encountered frog symbolical?

FROG
> *(to herself)*

This can be no coincidence!
That intellect universal
Learned omni-voracional
Politician-enigmatic
Aesthetician-expert-critic
Famed ass multilateral?!

DONKEY
> *(bowing in greeting)*

Madame…

FROG

    (bowing in greeting)
Monsieur…

SUN

    (to himself)
Like two peas in a pod, in fact —
To beasts from the same zodiac.

    (The donkey gazes long at the frog through his monocle. The frog gazes long at the donkey through her lorgnette)
Suddenly a huge blue fly buzzes onto the stage.

FLY

    (flitting about)
Zzer… zzer… zzer…
I'm searching for him…

    (The donkey, the frog and the sun pay no attention to the fly zooming about)

DONKEY

    (to frog)
I know already with whom I have the pleasure…

FROG

    (to donkey)
I know already with whom I have the honour…

SUN

    (to himself)
Idiots both they are
And I must shine for them.

FLY

    (buzzing around the donkey)
Ah something pleasant, tasty, meets

My nose here, something cloying-sweet…
Perhaps his pocket hides a treat?

THE FLY
        steals up on the donkey from the rear, armed with a long needle.

DONKEY
        (to frog)
To speak with you, madame, is such a rare delight…
Allow me to tender my respects, if I might…
        (he extracts a calling card from his wallet)
A donkey I; to say that caste of mine
Is of the rank patrician-asinine,
Is false-modest. We're writ up since the times
Of Plato, Aesop, LaFontaine, Krasicki,
Prokesch, Pieńkowski, Pietrzycki
Irzykowski, Haecker and Kozicki.

SUN
        (to himself)
He's really quite an interesting ass.

FROG
        (extracting a card from her purse and presenting it to the donkey)
I am a cabaret-frog, poetess,
Romano-novelo-essayist,
And avant-ou-après cyclist,
Pianisto-modernist,
Futuristic-dadaist,
Who likes humidity, ponds and bogs,
Mist and Venice canal-fogs.

DONKEY
I'm frequently found in the dailies…
That is, my deft critical sallies…
        (hoofing through the papers)

FROG
Surely you've heard much of frogs
Melancholic, arch-inquisitive,
Demonstro-committee-socio-visitive…
You'll see, sir, as we pursue our dialogue
More than one ass has heard of this worldly frog.

DONKEY
Surely you've read my articles:
Economico-politico-
Lyri-didactico-
Poetico-filo-
Arche-rubbish-istical…

FROG
Surely you know my poetry;
Szmaja is my publisher —
The same who edits Staśko, he's
World-famed for cookbooks and brochures…

SUN
And so I rise above Mount Helicon.

DONKEY
You'll find my name in Orgelbrand's lexicon.

FROG
My verses were critiqued by Szukiewicz.

DONKEY
And I was written up by Bartoszewicz.

FROG
With such delight did Hoesick wag
His beard over my volume,
He pronounced:
My poetry was written in perfume.

DONKEY
      (proudly)
My prose has a classical rhythm and form.

DONKEY
      (completely ravished by the donkey)
Apostle! Maestro! Divine abnorm
Al efflorescence of genius!

SUN
This dialogue of yours constrains us
To say — had we a hat, well — chapeau bas!

FROG
      (tossing her arms around the donkey's neck in delight)
Dear ass, desire's burning through my veins —
Bind us, Sun, in love's sweet eternal chains!
(Meanwhile the wanton fly, who up until now had been buzzing around the stage, stings the ass in the rear with her needle)
Startled at the sudden sharp pain, the donkey kicks out and brays:

        ua,   ua,   ua

FROG
      (in fright)
Oh my!
You're not having a heart attack?!

DONKEY
      (braying, kicking out)
Again that god-damned fly
Has made her way inside my frock!

FLY
      (buzzing around the stage)
Zhu — zhu — zhu
Ah! the ass brought an end to my sweet siesta,
Just as I was sniffing out a delicious fiesta!

. . . .

>   (*The Sun has stopped*
>   *The Frog's gone speechless*
>   *The Donkey kicks out, runs about*
>   *The Fly buzzes and wheels*)
>   Then an old haycock makes its appearance, at which a
> general silence falls.

HAYCOCK
>   (*advancing slowly*)
> Hearkenin' from afar to what yous said
> I came to stuff some wisdom in my poor head.
> I's just an ordinary village haycock
> What stands out in the field around the clock
> Burnt by the sun and battered in foul weather
> Bored through by rooks aimin' to dry their feathers.

. . . .

SUN
>   (*to himself*)
> That's all we needed! This strange sort of bird,
> To make our story all the more absurd.

DONKEY
>   (*to haycock, sentimentally*)
> Thou Polish haycock! Ah!
> Thy sweet odour of straw
> Reminds me, in sooth,
> Of the can-cans of my youth
> When, a little donkey at my sire's side
> I did my best to keep pace with his stride
> As we trod the paths of my youth
> To and fro my coltish stable-booth.
>   (*he approaches the haycock slowly*)

SUN
> *(to himself)*

Ubi genus ubi rura
Sic asinum vocat natura.

DONKEY

O thou hay familial,
This very spring from furrow culled,
Most tasty of all grass!
> *(bites the haycock)*

HAYCOCK

Roll up closer, my dear ass.
Now, don't be shy, my donkey! Do
Take 'ee a nice mouthful or two…
. . . .
An' you volks — look an' zee
Just how gen'rous an haycock mid be…
> *(Suddenly the haycock comes unbound. A stout field hand appears from within, gripping a whip and a rope. He tosses the rope around the donkey's neck and lays on with the whip)*

DONKEY
> *(roaring)*

Oyoyoy!
Gods of Olympus, aid me now! For here,
Of a sudden, is my old lord severe!

> *(With a splash, the Frog leaps into the pond*
> *The Fly buzzes off*
> *The Sun looks down in wonder)*

SUN
> *(sententiously)*

Strike not, bad man, the poor donkey!
This is the twentieth century!
Free him to fly now, like the brisk

Wind, or I'll ring the curtain down
On this burlesque,
And whistling, the alarm I'll sound
And summon aid, calling down
Those strapping futuresques,

Młodożeniec and Jasieński,
Stern and Wat, even Czyżewski.

FUTURIST
    (shouting from the house)
I'd like to come and help, but I can't move my feet.
A certain bitter critic's bound them to my seat!

FIELD HAND
    (tauntingly)
Eh... please!
Now Mr Sun keep your nose right where
It's wanted — up there in the air —
Worry 'bout heavenly broils and roustabouts,
Comets and planets or the Milky Way
Or those herrant stars that tend to stray...
But if you got to stick your snout
In things of earth — how 'bout them futurists?
Round 'em up, an' send 'em off to Pilec
An' leave me an' my jackass alone
F'r all hell's sake. This ass I own —
I bought 'im f'r a hunnert Polish marks,
Even if he goes off on those crazy larks,
Full of — what d'ye call it? — ambition.
An' that's just stupid. An ass a politician?
An' yet he prances round the village, impressin'
Bigger asses than 'isself.
But me? I hain't dim!
You just wait — I'll teach you a lesson!
    (Beats the donkey with the whip)

DONKEY
May God not hold this against
You — stifling all my talents!
But know this, however, wherever, whenever I get the chance
I'll do my best to wrest myself out of your cruel hands!
    (The rope breaks, the donkey escapes)

SUN
    (sententiously)
Fie on you yokel, to torment that poor ass!
When civil rights spread among us so, at last.
Freedom is here, and your rights now are shrunk. We
See how you're threatened by the eight-hour donkey!

FIELD HAND
    (to sun)
Yer more full of it than my yoke o' bulls!
Keep your own nose clean. Don't worry about me;
Even if that ass et all the talents for lunch
He's still an ass, sleeps in a stall, and basta!
    (exits)

SUN
    (to himself)
And ass is an ass — a field hand's nothing more
Than a profiteer's lackey. On that score,
They're both stupid. But better far, for sure
To be a profiteer or labourer
Than an intellectual-donkey snob…
    (looking out into the house)
But wait — what's that I see?
The moon's crept in among the toffs
Where ladies wait with champagne and candy!
So that's his game?
Well, I can do the same…
I'll take my aeroplane
To get there faster… *(whistles)*
Here he comes, like a dog to his master.

(An aeroplane flies in, picks up the sun and flies off)
(The distant croaking of frogs is heard)
A red twilight
The fly reenters
Reeling — she's drunk.

FLY
I can't recall, since I was very young,
Ever sipping such sweet mead, sweet and strong...
      (falls and gets up again)
Pardon — I didn't mean no
Disrespect — that's not like me, you know...
. . . .
Now, how to get myself a sinecure
Like the ass that stumbled into literature?

THE END

                                            (1918)

A Burglar of the Better Sort

One Act (10 minutes)

(1922)

Persons:

BURGLAR
GUEST
INGÉNIEUR DU MÉTROPOLITAIN (MANNEQUIN)
MIMI
ENTREPRENEUR

The salon of a cocotte in Paris.

A salon with smooth bare walls. Windows on the sides — larger to the front, smaller to the rear. On stage, instead of a prompter's booth, stands a huge gramophone. In one (rear) corner of the room stands a tailor's dummy. There are two doors. Dusk — some light seeps in from the streetside window.

The door to the left opens, and the **burglar** *enters. He is dressed in a dinner jacket, as if he was just returning from Café Bullier. He sweeps the room with an electric torch, as if he were searching for someone.*

A safe stands in the centre of the room. He picks the lock, opens it, and extracts a skull. He drops the skull on the floor. It makes a loud crunching noise; from it a string of pearls spills out.

Suddenly, offstage, a rooster crows loudly, twice.

A clock begins striking twelve, just as loudly.

A door, heretofore unseen, giving onto another room, opens. The stage fills with red light. The door is slammed shut. Enter the **guest.**

GUEST
> *(takes out his wallet, counts his banknotes:)*
Two hundred   three hundred
four hundred   one thousand
supper   three hundred
champagne   one hundred
taxi   one hundred
Mimi   one thousand

> *(Meanwhile, the burglar flattens himself against the wall in an attempt to hide)*

GUEST
> *(yawns)*
U… a… what a bore
it's almost day
time to hit the hay

> *From his place along the side wall, the mannequin (the Ingénieur du Métropolitain) moves toward the centre of the stage, with wooden strides. The clock strikes twelve again. A shimmy begins to spill out of the great horn of the gramophone at the front of the stage — the rooster crows three times*

MÉTROPOLITAIN
> *(walking about the stage with wooden strides, in time to the beat of the music and the tones of the striking clock)*

         One   two   three
     mon   sieur   gawks   at   ma   dame
 'tis   I   that   built   le   Mé   tro   po   li   tain
         Deep   un   der   Pa   ris
              hop   hop   hop

> *(The music stops playing)*
> The burglar and the guest assume

                the movements of the mannequin
(The music begins to play)
(The clock strikes 12, the rooster crows 3 times)
The mannequin, the burglar and the guest move around the room like wooden figures, rapping their heels.
The door through which the guest entered opens again —
enter Mimi the cocotte.

MIMI THE COCOTTE
      (in her dressing gown)
:   I am the cocotte named Mimi
I dance the cakewalk and the shimmy
a thousand francs   a thousand francs
pour une fois
      vive le roi
      (she displays her fingers as if illustrating the amount — then twirls on her own axis)

MANNEQUIN
I am the in   géneur
du Métro   poli   tain
I am that one and   **him**   just the same

GUEST
deux mille francs
pour deux fois
trop   cher   ma foi

BURGLAR
    (chloroformed)
    (gazes at the pearls)
Well today I made some bread
and my browning's full of lead
my pockets full of pearls
blood in my mouth foams and swirls
    (he shoots his browning in the direction of the audience)
    (Again music sounds from the gramophone)
    (the rooster crows — the clock strikes the hours)

(Everyone on stage join hands and dance in a ring to the beat of the music.
From among the audience a masked entrepreneur comes on stage. The music stops — no more dancing)

ENTREPRENEUR
Look at that will you folks
here we have modernity quite modern
burglars   floozies
guests and   mannequins
the guest pays, certainly
but nobody wins
and nobody loses.
I am an entrepreneur
I'm the one that earns
francs dollars pounds money to burn
from the work that you do
Mimi — isn't that true?

MIMI
    (in a high shrill voice)
yes   yes   yes

ENTREPRENEUR
        Yes   my   gentlemen
        oui   mes   dames
        ha   ha   ha
        civilisation   plutocracy
        democracy
    pornography   ethnology
Propedeu-tics   european   culture
    limps   tic   tic   tic
    four kings on the throne
      and four beneath it
      and satan snores
    (addresses the audience)
    at the tile stove's foot
but it's high time now an end to put

                    to this melodrama
                  hey burglar, come on
                 what're you waitin' for?
                          Shoot!

(The burglar takes out his browning and shoots, killing the guest, the mannequin, and at last himself. Only the entrepreneur and Mimi are left standing)

ENTREPRENEUR
:   have you eaten supper Mimi?!

MIMI
Yes!

ENTREPRENEUR
Did he shoot them already?

MIMI
Yes!

ENTREPRENEUR
And did he pay?!

MIMI
Yes!

ENTREPRENEUR
With effect or without?

MIMI
Yes!

ENTREPRENEUR
And two stiffs in the basement?

MIMI
Yes!

ENTREPRENEUR
Hypnotised?

MIMI
Yes!

ENTREPRENEUR
The Ingéneur du Métropolitain, he's calm today?

MIMI
Yes!

ENTREPRENEUR
    (takes Mimi around her waist)
Come along Mimi to the alcove
on the springy mattress we'll make love
and you'll show me all right
how much you earned tonight
at the bottom of it all my true delight
I pluck from trees in my own grove
counting the francs and making love
and you there, lying on the floor
    (to the corpses)
get up, corpses, and dance some more

    (he opens the door and goes off to the alcove with Mimi)
    The gramophone music plays, the clock strikes, the rooster crows.
    The corpses get up, join hands and dance.

(1921)

Night – Day

The Mechanical Instinct Electric

(1922)

Night – Day

day		arises and
night		disappears
wheels	rims	spin

	LIGHTNINGS	
dance	dance	dance on
day		dawns
night		departs

	NEBULAE	
blaze	emanate	style
aeroplane	wings	whirr
gigantic		day
and faint		night
hands	labour	work

	SPARKS	
burn	abrade	explode
and day		smoulders
and night		crows

	NAILS	
bleed	weep	cross

TYTUS CZYŻEWSKI

DE PROFUNDIS

PART I. THE GOLDEN SNAKE

    Ratata
        rata-ta
        ratata

. . . .

I opened the window
of my stuffy
        room
        to the world
naiads from the bosom of the sea
        emerge
hippy naiads
        cyclades
I ache to see you
        shining
        pining
        chiming
        desiring
bread   bread   bread
        and the gospel

. . . .

in sum
what was to become
became flesh among
us
    to dwell

. . . .

and the mountain trombones
blared the sea lanterns shone
grasshoppers intoned
their songs orange winds blew
arms and legs grew
stiff green the vales bloomed
        hey sweet girl hey

. . . .

hey sweetheart hey
come out girl and play
and bring your harvest scythe
soon you'll be a bedded bride
. . . .
Ah you youngsters have no fear
you that pouch and lyre bear
you'll be given hatchets here
and the burgeoning fecund sward
will bear you a meet reward
. . . .
       The parasols of the clouds fly
       to field descending from on high
       upon the cockle corn to lie
. . . .
      Above the rivers spin
           nightingales
    dizzy siskins
and the goldfinch
in the wooden vales
brassy a capella
     cello *chella*
in the cities
roll the wheels
black gold red
machines rabid
drink roar and tease
. . . .
    blazing cities
    blazing hair
  water lilies
. . . .
    the nights are dark
    the lanterns flare
pantries stallions
    of a golden carriage
    fabled manes
    wigs big brains

. . . .
and silence in the swales
and sheep on the steep vales
across the summits
gales gales
  blazing
. . . .
the Elevation silence growing
in the summer windborne sowing
barns fill with tears this year's yield
the flocks of sheep about the field
        going
. . . .
The heart of life booms like a gong
The sun comes up afire at dawn
stars earth months
the bow the strings creaks
about the linden hum the bees
. . . .
Jesus wept in misery
our woe He took upon Him He
rests in chapel and sacristy
     He's
at crossroads and
on winter nights frozen
He weeps
     O Jesus!!
. . . .
    there in the maytime valley
    the bells of violets jangle
and the galanthus bells
    as well
    little angels
. . . .
about my chambers now
till golden harrow and plough
round my churches are found, all
gold icons of Mary on the wall

smouldering burning sputtering
fainting tottering
. . . .

        Blessed be the Lord
                Jesus Christ
        Now and forever
            Amen
. . . .
and in sum
He who was to become
Flesh became coming among
us to dwell
. . . .
        Behold my verbal
              primatiae
      lance-like words
             bloody birds
      trunk hands and head
            Words Words
. . . .
Trunk head and hands
            sanctificans

PART II. SPRING

The hum of automobile tyres
        An aeroplane zips
        in a frenzied rush
He went he lay down in a tomb
            and perished
        The concierge
        The old suicide
And on that day
           it was said unto me
that Christ had been asking after me
but I was not at home

And on that day
        it was said unto me
that Satan had been asking for me
but I was not at home
And Judas came along
and paid me thirty silver pieces
Simon and Cleophas
at the same time it was
were on their way to Emaus
and who met up with them but Lord Jesus
        Alleluia!
and bells bells bells
        all the bells
And my father following the plough
spring following the plough
        in the springtime springtime
And my mother going to the fields
        in the springtime springtime
And the bells going to the fields
        in the springtime springtime
And all the birds fly to the fields
        in the springtime springtime
Hours days months years
and ages go into the fields
        in the springtime springtime
And they stopped and about they gazed
and sang and whistled O happy days
They played on fiddle bass and flute
on horn and clarinet to boot
they joined their hands and danced about
and sang and whistled the happy rout
Then came Mażana in the spring
Set up her loom the warp to string
Mażana came the virgin girl
Dziewanna of the golden curls
My sweetheart's on his way indeed
and to his bed he will me lead
he's riding on a small grey horse

behind him rides a vast armed force
And then they stopped about them gazed
and sang and whistled O happy days
They played on fiddle bass and flute
on horn and clarinet to boot
He met me on the 'avenue
   de la grande Armée'
Judas asking 'when will you
be home?' and then the hour struck
upon the white tower clock
the propeller buzzed
and I met four coffins along my route
the tramway ran over
             the ragman's cart
And I walked on the street and thought

    CINQ BIS (5 bis)
Judas will come by
and buy a few paintings
      and
        the propeller
      buzzed
          and
      the fields
     flew
and bells bells
            and
          Spring
And they stopped and about they gazed
and sang and whistled O happy days

Part III. A Waterfall of magnetic tears

holding hands at a distance
pianofortes sick suffering machines
the tears of old houses in the suburbs of war
the Spinning mills of fatal kisses
kisses of kissing cadavers' hands

everything a machine my pianoforte
slavic lyre bagpipes bleating
on mountains in valley in meadow
bleating away beside sheep bleating
. . . .
and I emerged with my hands full
of the dawn of kaleidoscopic urano-storms
of lightning bolts telegrams the souls of Morse
in speechless comprehension by otherworldly light
. . . .
and I emerged with my eyes full
down the slopes of dusty roads leading in all four directions
of tenements pregnant hospitals of prostitutes
immaculate through the hysteria of purity of wombs
of blooms glowing of burning steam-churches
praying over Sabbath Szabaśniki
of witches of those prostrate pronelying pro-domos
(l'avion de mon corps adoré)
. . . .
(mon cor criant dans le bois)
. . . .
and I emerged with my mouth full of clavichords
and the dissonance of sonata sonatina hydro-storm
of curses musky snakes of rubber
boxes selfincindiary fires conflagrations
waterfalls of tears athirst for the lilies of southern valleys
of midwife setting afire a vale of hearts
of welcoming wide-stretching seas electric
electrons of moaning big-breasted Electra
of love rings on an open bed
I emerged with my thoughts full
at the early hour of blackcocks at dawn
I with the silence of blazing avalanche
lava I listen to whispers of sunlit nature
and now I've emerged at the wound on my arm
where I pinned two sail-arms slimy and sounding
   I go   and I go   and I go   I

Part IV. Coral

The swallow black and white
painted its nest built
the stork and the summer oriole
yellow and white artists
then came the electric wave
to rest upon a butterfly's wing
and then it flew across the oceans
out flew the flying fish
singing themselves cavorting
and the sirens did themselves up coral and sepia
then came the idols of **taka-huhu**
sculptures crocodiles turtles
and hummingbirds made up with thin brushes
in the mirrors of crimson lakes
and then came hypnotised
golden-turning birds of paradise
painting singing building the art of animals
    nests   feathers   wings
and then came I the artist
their pupil their medium their thrall Raphael
and I created a half hummingbird-bat
flying about the ceiling of my studio
chiming out the hours
singing courantes
but that wasn't the art I was looking for
so I went into the depths of waters electric
red-webbed and amber
and there I found work for these hands
a galvano-picture

- -

o star of seven colours
the greatest animal artist
I have become his pupil
rainbows northern dawns cyclones
magnetism instinct essentialism
give birth to me give birth to me give birth to me
                      (1920)

Monkeys in the Menagerie
(a nonsensical fable)

Once upon a time, it did befall
in a town become a nation's capital,
that a zoo was set up
with monkeys in a stall
and animals of all
different types well suited
to zoos, six- four- and two-footed;
all sorts of beasts indeed,
and none of them could read.

Monkeys: chee-reek…
katcha-hee-hee…
katcha-hee-hee…
. . . .
they jump they screech they swing around
and everything is turned upside-down
. . . .
(their cages reek)
when they seek
cooling, there's a creek
to hop into
with pirouette
and head
first dives
and thus the dusky monkeys live their lives
. . . .
Now, the other bestial folks
had enough of apish jokes
calm they were (truth be spoke)
Cut it out! they roared aloud
Such chaos is not allowed!
. . . .
As if their protests could stop
The monkeys, who still screech and hop!
. . . .

But then took voice an ass
who, though stupid, well-liked was
and he came up with a gay plan…
No monkey
said he
would leap and chee
if like the two-legged beast
his bright eyes he should feast
upon a looking glass
. . . .
the motion passed
and into the mitts
of each monkey was fixed
a mirror; each ape now sits
and gapes —
no more japes
from the apes!
. . . .
Now, all you who hear
my satire, draw near.
If you find
It's Warsaw I have in mind,
God forbid!
. . . .
These are just monkey-shines
fit for simian minds.

Sensation in the Movie-House

The Palace Kino: *Murder in Bombay*
oy vey   oy vey   oy vey   oy vey
four   trees   a car   the sea
the porter makes someone angry
Damn Ola Föns my nerves are wearing
thin This whole place reeks of herring
Hela's leg's bit by a flea
O look his teeth are so ugly
Someone's stood up, stands right in front of me

Hey born-in-a-sty I cannot see
Sit down there sir for goodness' sake
Mia May from the window takes
A dive God she'll land on her head

Dear Lord she's dead she's surely dead
four lackeys carry her inside
alive   alive   alive   alive
what a sensation At the break
the usher girls are hawking cakes
Whew Mia May just like a cat
nine lives Don't waste your dough like that
Hey stop your groping now come on
Can't you see the lights are still on
A drama full of mystery
He'll die? He'll live? Hold on we'll see
Ko-ko-ta laughs Where? Up there higher
Celluloid dust nerves smudge of mire

The Regiment
A Military Romance

10 soldiers were on guard duty
26 soldiers were in a van
34 soldiers were at the firing range
56 were eating dinner
9 went to the park with their nannies
the major was sipping black coffee
the major's wife was darning a stocking
the colonel was kissing the maid
the colonel's wife was frying scrambled eggs
the captain was pouring a drink
the corporal was saluting
the sergeant was saluting
the lieutenant was passing by
the lieutenant's fiancée was weeping
someone fired his Mauser
2 soldiers went to get the coffin

2 soldiers were on guard duty
2 soldiers carried out the colonel
the orderly carried round the orders
2 soldiers were conversing
the colonel's wife was weeping
the major was sipping black coffee
the captain's wife was weeping
the captain put his sword belt on
the military chaplain sang

. . . .

(The end)

The Ballad of Kitty the Waitress

So at a café in the city
I first met the waitress Kitty
cappuccino, café au lait
sugar and lemon on a plate
two fingers snap — a Second Louie
wants ginger-snaps for his girl Zoe
Kitty Kitty please our bill
Auntie Mama Auntie shrill
the clatter in the small café
where Kitty bustles round all day
the Captain lounges spreadingly
and ogles Kitty brazenly
Now Now No pinching captain or
the tray will spill out on the floor
Tomorrow then you'll come to me
I'll give you a fur coat you'll see
Let go the siphon O you're droll
you see you're stopping up my hole
No never no no not like that
'I'd like to pay Miss Kitty Cat'
who's calling for the tab O that's
the confidential clerk named Katz
– – coming coming on my way
there's only one of me today

check please check please we'd like to pay
Dear Lord I'm going nuts I say
- - - - - - - - - - - - - - - - - -

Café au lait a little roll
Give me a kiss Kitty you doll
Now now you mustn't stroke my legs
Miss Kitty please some scrambled eggs
'two portions of two scrambled eggs'
'Figaro for me, for me the Gazette
And a cigar. Or cigarette.'
- - - - - - - - - - - - - - - - - -

Tomorrow Kitty's got a date
'Kitty, make sure you're not out late'
Says Auntie (Day off, she's at home)
'don't let Józek get you alone'
we're only going to the show
(she lives with Auntie now you know
and this Józek is Kitty's beau)
Jesus and Mary Kitty it's
three in the morning Auntie sits
up in the bed and rubs her eyes
after the show the girls and guys
went out for coffee Kitty lies
Shivering through her dreams that night:
I can't I won't Józek I might.

Dozing in the Café

In the warm silent café three

. . . .

Idiots sit down to black coffee

. . . .

In their brackets drowse electric tapers

. . . .

The idiots are reading the papers

. . . .

Three dolts nourished by 'Check Mate'

. . . .

The 'Warsaw Courier' and 'The State'
. . . .
In the buffet a clatter of plates
. . . .
A flush of water in the jakes
. . . .
Somewhere they're frying chops and capers
. . . .
The idiots are reading papers
. . . .
In the aromatic silence here
. . . .
From time to time there meets the ear
. . . .
The mumbling of four profiteers
. . . .
On sugar shipments it appears
. . . .
Next to the window light-bulb tapers
. . . .
Three idiots are reading papers
. . . .
The newest dope on Bundesliga
. . . .
Trotsky and Sapieha in Riga
. . . .
Above the ceiling fan is sweeping
. . . .
Below three idiots lightly sleeping
. . . .
You'd say such is the atmosphere
. . . .
That all is catatonic here
. . . .
The forks are snoring the knives drowse
. . . .
The café waiters and who knows
. . . .

Perhaps even the Sukiennice
. . . .
Nods drowsily as do Ulice
. . . .
Szewska Długa Wolska and
. . . .
All of drowsing drained Poland.

SHE DIDN'T KNOW

He chauffeur and she — seamstress
A so-so more or less seamstress
O she loved him loved him so
o lala lalala lalala
Along the street he drove and tooted
tudu tudu tudu
At her machine she sat and sewed
She only lived for him you know
She loved him O she loved him so
O lala lalala lalala
But once she cheated on her guy
Never trust women how they lie
Despite the fact she loved him so
O very much she loved him O
Lala lalala lalala
You think he shot himself in the head?
Or her or his rival instead?
For after all she loved him so
O lala lalala la no
He laughed he drove his car and tooted
tutu tutu tutu - -
She sat there weeping as she sewed
Because she loved she loved him so
O lala lala lalala
(You thing she was sewing made to order?)
It was a little tiny sort o'
Shirt she sewed in love but who
She knew not who more of the two

O boo-hoo boo-hoo boo-hoo-hoo
Because she loved them both loved two
But which one more she knew not who
O la lalala la boo-hoo.
                    (1919)

The Assumption
(An idyll)

The height of summer on its way
golden the cornfield grows
The gravid stalks seed-heavy sway
Fodder in sweet-smelling windrows
And varied blooms in holt and hurst
Gather them up, and bind them all
Into wreaths of gold blue and green
An offering to the Virgin Queen.
The custom today as 'twas at first:
          In short, a pastoral.
. . . .
The bells bong out for the High Mass…
in shawls of red, in chequered skirts
the women clad, dark-coloured vests
Or in white shirts
the peasants walk on smartly dressed
Gossip greets gossip as they pass.
Here's more than one homey hint or
Subject for painting: the old church
With its sifting planks of larch
The ancient organ squealing like scald-
-ed cats, the naive sermon of the bald
Old priest (so old he won't see winter)
The grey hair of the peasants gleams
As over their prayerbooks they nod
A lovely sight, by God —
Themes for a nice bucolic scene.
. . . .
And after Mass the Church erupts

             in gay cacophony…
The peasants' pied vests
             In the sun…
And the local toffs too, every one
Of the landlords, father son
And uncle, were in church today
. . . .
in the tavern of the side-curled Jew
a crowd of people at the bar
discussing what the landlord said:
Let all the peasants gather
at the manor house on Sunday
Whoever's looking to buy land or rather
some forest parcel, for his sake or
someone else's; the lord is splitting
his land up, for an acre
a pretty penny he'll be asking
This is why they're sitting
quarrelling rehashing
This fellow, leader of the band
he'd like to be, it seems, starts yelling
Friends friends listen together we stand
What's it to us this buying and selling
All for one boys this is our land
. . . .
The summer day's fled
The sun goes down the corn glows red
aspen leaves shimmering
become like the glimmering
Sun as the evening comes on
the Day of Mary's Assumption
Which calmly ebbs to peace.
. . . .
at once the melancholy moon
trims his sad lantern…
. . . .
The cottage yards reek of manure…
roses cense the orchard trees

Someone opens the tavern door
A snatch of song flits on the breeze

(1903)

Forest

The forest bristles the hill's brim
the breeze makes sway its rows of columns
they sing to Nature a soft hymn
before they drowse again in solemn
quiet; but soon the litanies
begin anew; birds ring carillons
the forest murmurs as the trees
pray pray for us pray for us on and on
across the heavens roll a flock
of clouds the firs stand silent, dim
the woods, above the clouds are rocked
below sing unknown violins.

(1902)

Medium

Soft sounds like the odours of rusty blooms
the melodies of dried roses that bring to mind pummelled cruses
nightmare and dread glide forth from perfidious tombs
their gait is weak and solemn as befits aeolian shades
proud husbands lead their wives the lovely saffian oxygen erotic
disappear — harp string and murmur fade
 living veins currents electric
the rhythmic tones cease the tender thrum
this I beheld magnetic medium
11 November in the afternoon 1914.

In the Mental Ward

    Right hand   wave of gold   Thought   Thoughts
    left hand   a silver wave   there flash celadon
                   wheels of green   clouds
                   two   Here comes my mate he stands
                                              at the gate
a tangle of snakes copper thoughts
writhing along the sidewalk   a - a - a - a
ding ding ding   two little cats both dun and grey
Two Little Kittens   Lost Their   Mittens
        four   and now who goes is
Me brassy candlesticks
metempsychosis
      Sister   brother   I'm off to dress up God
        Sister of mercy   at his bed
white wings   I'm off to the kitchen instead
      the rooster's head   in Paradise
Two white handrails   Bowls of ivory
      faded eyes   Plates of abalone
And the eyelashes of iron bars Good morning to you God
they're closing down my day   Doctor sir
day day day   Good day

(1920)

Mechanical Garden

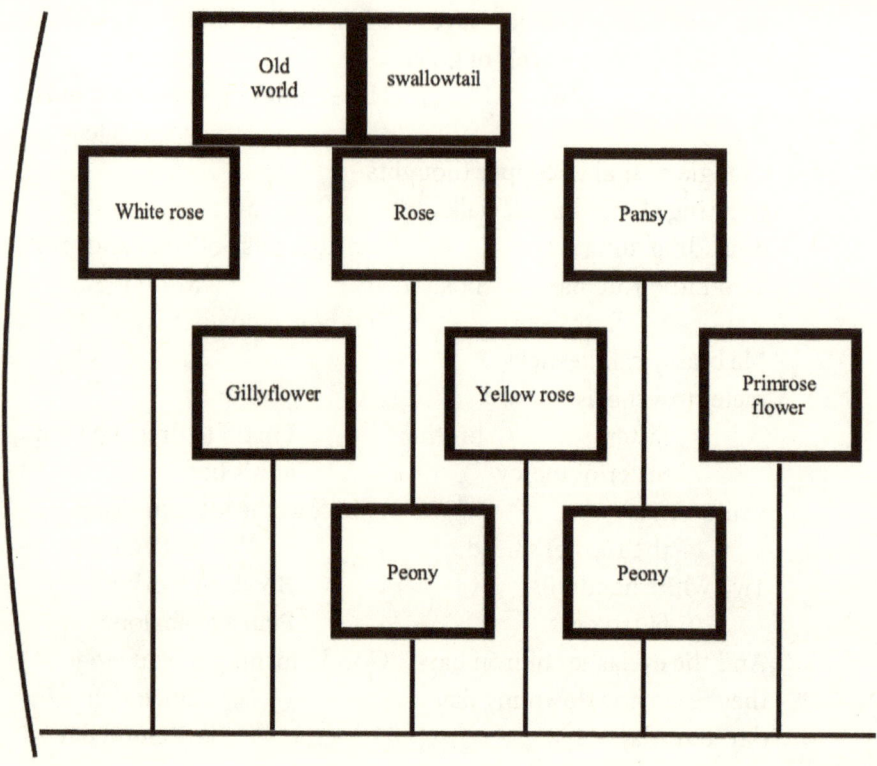

```
     Dawn         Dew                 Dogrose
   sun         sunflowers       mountains     afar
 butterfly    swallowtail                  yellow roses
    the grass is laughing                   the sun
       is laughing         and           i and my hope
```

(1920)

RETURN

Where are you flying it's so late
(it's twelve o'clock at night)
my brother cranes my sister wild geese
my friends the swans
glide away glide away through the heavens
amongst the starry islands
to the golden isles of an azure sea
Tomorrow you may rest at dawn
dip your feathers into a pearlescent sea
I'm flying along with you my dear birds
into the autumn night amongst the stars
gripping your wings I am
(wretched earthworm as I am
having no feathers of my own)
tomorrow at this same late hour
we'll fly amidst some new stars
like the ship of an explorer
I have rested my hands upon the mountaintops
I feel their summits with my palms
like the nipples of a woman's breasts
beneath my fingers' electric current
I've seized a giant bird with my hands
and thus I grip him
Bear me off with you bird into Wyraj
where in the wilds black-hung with creepers
at the foot of a dry-crumbling cliff
a seed of radium glows
like a firefly, and then
bear me off
to a timeless monstrous evergreen wood
in the thickets of which rests
MY GREAT GRANDDAD THE GORILLA
sipping water from the bowl of
      ELECTRIC NATURE
at his side I wish to become primordial
just as I was a thousand ages ago.

Trapdoor

   I walk
along long pavements
   through corridors
through dark basements
through carillon peals
through lambent fields
through thoughts uncertain
through crimson curtains
through rooms of larch
through steppes pale-blanched
I walk through sounds
through fiddle strings
   that fly
   before me
. . . .
   I've walked
into yellow rooms
their doors all locked
   and bound
into soft sounds
songs of rosy sheen
and tapestries of green
. . . .
45 chambers
45 doors
45 keys
45 thresholds
all locked
all locked
   before me
. . . .
I walk through dark basements
I walk along narrow pavements
   I enter
a deep corridor
   and I
     fall

into crimson water
a depthless abyss
      a velvet canvas
         without a bottom
. . . .
a fire is
lit tallow
candles tallow sallow countenance
hands iris
the fire is candles tallow
      abyss abyss
        without a
. . . .
a   a   a
. . . .
I recognised the eyes
zooming along the hotel lift
in the sweltering afternoon
      to the bottom
. . . .
basements pavements
iris fire is
      tallow
fires sharp spires
abyss abyss
      without a bottom.

The Flame and the Well
(electro-kino-aero-dramo)

        (a screen and a well)
    on the screen — clouds — a sea
          two ships
   In the depths of the green well
      A dynamo in motion
       electric dancing
        a propeller

A HOUSE
(that stands nearby)
Opens its sparking window

   Smoke   Smoke   Smoke
(on the screen)
Electro-machines dancing
Electro-worlds dancing
   Sun   Sun   Sun
(pauses above the well)
Don Juan:
(emerges from the well)
(a naked manikin electro-corpse)
: I seduced Donna Alvarez
the galvanised manikin
electro-corpse
of a woman :
(rises from the well)
(the galvanised corpse)
(electro-manikin)
(of Donna Alvarez)
Donna Alvarez:
: I'm giving birth to a child-corpse —
electro-manikin
Don Juan
(galvanised manikin —)

(electro-corpse)
(laughs aloud)
: ha   ha   ha   ha
An Aeroplane
(falls from the sky)
(the propeller hums)
(its gigantic magnet)
(draws upward)
(the galvanised)
(manikin corpses)
everyone falls into the well
THE HOUSE
(closes its window)

on the screen:
two
orange roses
(there arises from the well)
(a shining banner)
(upon which is written) :
**: there are no laws
in all of nature
there is only one great
mechanical**

electrical instinct
alone
ha   ha   ha   ha
Sun   Sun   Sun

(1921)

Hymn to the machine of my body

blood   pepsin   blood
stomach   heart   blood
pulse   beat   the fixed
scrolls   of my   guts
               brain

cables to my veins   one   one   one
the twisted wire of the ducting   beats my heart hum hum
to my heart   my electric heart thrums
the battery
have mercy on me   o transmission belt
my **heart**   of my **guts**
dynamo-heart   two   two   two
electric lungs
magnetic diaphragm   have mercy on me
thoracic   one two

telephone of my brain
dynamo-brain
three   three   three
one   two   three
o machine of my body
function spin
live.

(1920)

Clairvoyant-Mechanical photograph of the poet Bruno Jasieński

(taken by the light of the guillotine)

taka-hu   **taka-hu**
the spectral flames are burning
long hands are strolling about the room next door
the brain is full of snakes and at this moment may be found
in the kitchen on a frying pan
grand amethyst eyes are swimming about
along with the Christmas Eve carp in the bathtub
long lunatic legs are descending from the sofa
and creeping up on the commode
fingers at this moment are playing on a clavichord
'god save the King'
the spine is brimming with electrical current
the lungs break and rot in the chest
each individual hair seeks out the ducts of telephone chimes
the heart stops beating
and is at this moment
in the chalice in the tabernacle
you speak to me in your sleep
you tell me that you're in the vault
of a gothic cathedral
that you're ceasing to live
drowning in orange water
I wake you up   I wake you up
I set up the camera
switch on the light of the magnetic dawn
and I see your brow
lit up askance by the light of the inferno
I bathe the film in golden water
fixing the image to bromopaper
conjuring your spectral face

(from the clairvoyant-magnetic photographic atelier of Tytus Czyżewski)

Genius and Doppelgänger

A scene beyond the senses — the stage is a gigantic skull. The jaw is dropped, one can see the interior of the skull, the empty eye sockets (white skull, black background).

The genius stands in the centre of the skull the doppelgänger to the rear, leaning against the inside wall of the skull. } black silhouettes

GENIUS
thoughts   threads   tangled   open mouth
    brain brain silence   night lamp

DOPPELGÄNGER
lamp lamp lamp
    I am great
        a Bell

GENIUS
I can't see I see
    it flies it flies a wing of white

DOPPELGÄNGER
my wing
    my thoughts

GENIUS
I see god
    sitting throne stars   angels
        archangels   rainbows

DOPPELGÄNGER
once more I've seen
    my greatness greatness
        alone

GENIUS
I am   small   small   please
      hands folded I love   dust

DOPPELGÄNGER
my   thoughts   are   me
       unplumbed   sublime
                  higher than   he

GENIUS
(stretches out his hands)
      o   o   o

DOPPELGÄNGER
(stretches out his hands)
      o   o   o

GENIUS
(casts himself down, his arms spread crosswise)

DOPPELGÄNGER
(stands, his arms spread crosswise)

GENIUS
(gets up slowly, spreads his arms crosswise)

DOPPELGÄNGER
(slowly lets his arms fall to his side)

GENIUS
I see I'm shivered by a star

DOPPELGÄNGER
God   Himself   goes   me   He

(there walks slowly about in the skull)
(a great black rat)

GENIUS
What   I have   pondered
             returns to   me   shining

DOPPELGÄNGER
he's coming   to   me

GENIUS
I see   everything   fire

DOPPELGÄNGER
I see   nothing   night

GENIUS
I   experience

DOPPELGÄNGER
he   sees

(the rat goes slowly the Doppelgänger)

GENIUS
I pass by   I'll go   I'll pass away
(goes slowly)

GENIUS
who   goes after   me goes
let   him   go

DOPPELGÄNGER
I won't go   I don't believe   fear

GENIUS
he's   going out   of me

(rat nearer Doppelgänger)

GENIUS
o

DOPPELGÄNGER
o

GENIUS
the star   flies   falls
    into   my   brain

DOPPELGÄNGER
lies   lies   ha
    God   is   no

    (a shattering sound and a whistle)
  (a lightning bolt bores through the skull)
      (rat Doppelgänger disappear)

GENIUS
(spreads his arms crosswise)
I believe in what
    I believe
and so   I go

(a green light in the skull)
    (the GENIUS goes)
(the huge jaw of the skull)
    (shuts)
                         (1920)

Transcendental Panopticum

everything's fluttering hankies
flags flagons filigreed
teacups lajkoniks like ostriches
barbarian tawdry beauties shacks
waterclosets of nature of super-sense
    wax figures
murderers geniuses generals
with electro-chromatic implements
a windup mickiewicz
writes an ode to youth
with a wig of curls artificial
tegetthoff the admiral
lunettes sail ships
blossoms bloom puffer fishes butter dishes
rippers   murderers
hunchbacks brainiacs pickpockets
degenerated chamber pots
of the applied arts
    figures of wax
    figures of wax
dance animated by electricity
dance in loving pairs super-manikins
minuet mazurka marengo marino
mannequins ta ta ta monoliths
maria theresa   tsar pavel   catherine
king edward   prince poniatowski
napoléon   ibsen
rollicking   rolling
enmanniquined galvanised
beside a behemoth   electromechanical
elemental   instinctual
pianol- a   auto   gramophone
    ta-rah
    electrical panoptical genius
        (dances)
:   i dance a minuet of memories
tears and twisted backbones

electrical napoléon
           (wound-up dances)
:   i am a holocaustical genius
strumming the mandolin of the ages
           panoptical mickiewicz
:   i have encompassed the electroglobe entire
all the wound-up stars dance along with me
hypnoticalmedium
               (sleep dances)
:   i behold a golden snake
in the depths of alcibiades' pocket
i behold instinctive animals
mating with the lightning bolts of electrons
         the panopticum director
                   (enters)
:   ladies and gentlemen
i the owner of the panopticum
beg the respected public
come come and see
behold the great napoléon
wound up innards automaton
behold electric mickiewicz
writing with magnetised pen
i have ordered   some new models
george sand   is on her way
:   an unknown soldier from Verdun
:   hamlet and ophelia
:   chopin a-dying
:   d'annunzio sleeping and rising
:   dante on electric current
come in   look around
the last   day   of the sensational
ultimatesunlit occasion
- - - - - - - - - - - - - - - - - - - -
         all the electromannequins
               (together)
we're lovemaking   lovemaking   lovemaking
        now   now   now

(Then all the sentimental bells ring out
of all the urano-churches
chapels cappellas of aether and warm
dawns stars primordial polar storms
  and
suns).
  the public and mannequins
    (together)
let's make love let's make love let's make love
magnetic corpses of the world we
  now   now now
let's impregnate give birth electrify
enmannequin the world
  director public mannequins
    (dance)
the electro-piano-barrelorgan
  plays

I:
as the creator
of the electro worlds of my brain
I medium unto myself
the first electro magnetic
poet and painter
tytus czyżewski
have hypnotised my thoughts
muddled through passed right through
the sententious sentimentalism
I enter life I create
swarms of electrons storms
in my brain
enacting art and hypnolaws
of the bestialised stars
of my electromedial instinct

        (1921)

The Watch

                21 hours says
                  my watch
passing along the edges of the street
              I catch my foot
against the door of a perruquier
        a new situation arises
and thus a new direction in poetry
           22 hours says
             my watch
passing along the edges of the boulevard
           I catch my head
against the leaves of a dry acacia
        from this nervo-situation
a new direction in painting comes about
          following in the pattern
     of my other great ancestors
        ancient antecedents
         plio- or ichthosaurus
       great cavern monkeys
            and
         their poetry
   mia   -   u
   mia   -   u
         their poetry
    chee   chee
          of snails
      gaily expectorating
         red saliva
 lee   lee   lee   lee
the barking of my forefather
            dog
   hyrr   rrr   rrr
I am like the harper of the street
          unknown
   spat upon unacknowledged

- -

> but now my watch says
> **2300 HOURS**
> on the rails on shock absorbent tracks
> my orient-express awaits
> **PACIFIQUE COMPANY**
> 2400 HOURS
> (in the vest pocket)
> (of my smoking jacket)
> (in my sleeping wagon)
> **the watch**

The Doll
(telephone)

To Andrzej Pronaszko

I'm hammering an interior
together boards screws and nails
painting it crimson and silver
inside I'm placing
two telephone lines
       the apparatus
upon the summit of the building
I fix the head of a **doll**
with rolling eyes
hallo   **hallo**
I am   undressed
       uncombed
hallo   hallo
and so goodbye
hallo   hallo
I've a bone to pick with you madame
ding   ding   ding   ding
       trrrr
lalo   lalo   lalo
   LAL
   DING

From the Machine to Animals

The sentimental epigones of romanticism and symbolism are dying away — a new era is dawning, with new values — and without the naive illusions of naive naturalism.

The elemental thrust — is from general mechanism **to the animal instinct** — we shall be brothers to the beasts and learn **instinctual art** from them, we shall love machines because they are our sisters, and animals because they are our mentors and brothers.

Just please no programmatic primitivities
 == instinct
let us kill the 'aestheticism' within us!
 Ladies and gentlemen, beasts of hearthside and the wilds,
 == the electric instinct
 (machine and element).

....

We love our electrical machines and we do them no harm.

....

We are learning music from the birds. — Architecture, painting and sculpture from the nests of beasts.

The mechanistic instinct == 'let each one write, sculpt and paint as his instinct directs him!'

We're in search of the **instinct** that we lost while perfecting ourselves in art and science over the course of so many centuries.

 Long live the electrical instinct
 the instinctual art of the animals
 the instinct electrical
 of the cosmos
 of minerals plants beasts men
 of the inner life of the **medium**.

Tytus Czyżewski on 'The Green Eye' and on his Painting
(Self-criticism — Selfadvertisement)

'The Green Eye' was written by Tytus Czyżewski, otherwise **me** musing on the perversity of colour, line and form. In this world, everything is alive and everything has its own particular value. What lives not — exists not, and what exists not has neither form nor hue.

'The Alleycat Serenade' I wrote while 'inspired' by the amorous longings of a certain tom cat belonging to an old acquaintance of a little kitten with whom I was acquainted.

Love among the beats is accomplished with furrore and the directness of **instinct.**

My **'Pastorals'** are the reminiscence of the village at the foot of the Tatras where I spent my childhood, upon which great quantities of snow fell in December
hey a-carolling a-carolling.

'Singing Houses' is a 'narrative poem' of crooked lines and measure. Everything dances in the lusty postwar European rut.

The houses laugh at people, and people weep at their own idiocy.

Children laugh at their parents.

'The Melody of the Crowd' is a narrative poem of unease, or the irritating mishmash of a Parisian boulevard (Boul-Michel) in which my personality happened to find itself (that of a Polish artist lacking both rudder and anchor).

'Le soir d'amour' is the chattering of teeth **before 'that'** — which **'later'** becomes something quite banal.

'Electric Visions' — a mechanised narrative poem.

Man inseminated and unleashed the machine, which one day will either kill him, or exalt him.

We build machines — we shall travel to the stars so as to observe the sun.

The sun will marvel at where man found so much 'understanding.'

Man will build a mechanical sun.

The old sun — is an honest old machine.

Let us love the sun and not talk about him behind his back.

The man of the future is an electrical machine — sensitive, complicated, and simple in style.

. . . .

Various critics wrote various things about 'The Green Eye.'

Those critics writing in newspapers about 'poetry' were in agreement, almost to a man, that my verses are constructed with a minimum of 'talent,' whereas they acknowledged my paintings to be of 'epochal' significance.

And, on the contrary — critics writing in newspapers about the **'plastic** arts' were in agreement, almost to a man, that my poetry is of 'epochal' (?!) significance, while my painting is 'infirm' lacking 'design' and 'colour.'

Knowing, however, from experience, that the best articles appearing in the Polish press on politics are written by engineers and musicians — on agriculture and horticulture — by generals, on economics — by poets, on poetry — by lawyers and physicians, on medicine — by professors of ancient tongues (greek, latin), on greek and latin — by professors of design, on the plastic arts — by veterinarians, geologists and political scientists,

For this reason I am **completely at ease** concerning both my 'Green Eye' and my painting.

Love electric machines, marry them and generate Dynamo-children — magnetise and educate them so that they grow to become mechanised citizens.

It is this that your poet without **'wings,'** your painter without **'colouring,'** desires on your behalf.

Pastorals

(1925)

Pastorals

A Carol

Ho ha hum
come shepherds come
hum ha ho
go shepherds go
to the crèche to the Virgin Mary
take your place by Joseph, where he
stands
near the crib or
manger, you
Grzegorz tallyman
provincial scribbler
you go too

hoo hoo hoo
come to the manger
that means you
slow-footed granger
get up from the pews
hop to it
Józek Suet
leave your alleys leave your mews
you, Franek, bleary
leave your mead your bread your stews
run to the manger, run to Mary

ho ha hum
come shepherds come
in from the fields in from the fold
I'm calling you, Janek the bold
take two rams you'll also need
two flagons of clove-scented mead
white cheese to match it
fiddles and hatchets
lutes and flails
what's that? I see the sly wolves' tails
oo — see them wheeling
your rams they're stealing
part of your yield
torn in the field
with crooked horns
of black wool shorn
meanwhile the shepherds far from danger
have gathered at the holy manger
to kneel before the straw-lined box
warmed by the breath of ass and ox
they greet the Maid they greet the Child
while all the birds from wood and wild
chirp gaily round the little bed
look at them as they bob their heads
while every shepherd hops and sings
the fiddlers bowing all their strings
twing twing twing twang barp barp barp
Kajtek's a-twanging his Jew's-harp
while Burek wags his tail and whimpers
gives his paw and pants and simpers
lullaby o lullaby
stop that you'll make the Baby cry
zum-zum the bow across the bass
scrapes, sweating the bassist wipes his face
zum-zum there in the manger where he
plays for the Babe and Mother Mary

and now three kings are kneeling down
three heads and on each head a crown
and there's a camel with a lump
footsore and knackered, well, he humped
a pretty mile to here from there
splendid the golden robes they wear
those wisemen from afar, those kings
and ah the gifts that each king brings
thalers of gold in treasure box
e moo e moo each wiseman talks
in his own tongue, his dialect
lee lee lee lee ee lee
as they inspect
the wondrous new-born Deity
in wonder they gaze at the Child
Who whimpers — ah, look how He smiled!
now all the shepherds genuflect
and all the beasts as well have kneeled
the bright star smiles above the field
glowing aloft in the night sky
and bending low it winks its eye
ah, it's so low above the shed!
the boors in fright duck low their heads
now lullaby o lullaby
see Mary cast a tender eye
upon her new-born Son, her Child
rocking His crib, His Mother mild

(1919)

Tiny Canticles

(the Birds of the Wood come near)

Over the hills throughout the vales
throughout the vales throughout the dales
the good news spread through the wide earth
about the Virgin giving birth
and all the birds O every one

flew to the crèche to see her Son
all the musicians of the dense
wood chatter now atop the fence
pigeons and doves that bill and coo
and mourning doves, wood pigeons too
the eagles and the falcons grey
chaffinches and woodpeckers gay
nuthatches and goldfinches play
the songsters of the woods, siskins

and pigeons

gru hoo gru hoo gru hoo
soft down beneath the Child's head strew
the eagles: he tweets he tweets
the siskins: so sweet so sweet
while the thrushes and the crows
fee fiu fee fiu
squawk like there's no tomorrow

(out of the manger to the birds
comes Old Joseph to have a word)

JOSEPH (to the birds)
ah, quiet now, be silent now
don't scream like that don't sing
the woods too small now, that you bring
your chatter here
so near
the Heavenly Child?

EAGLE (to Joseph)
old Lord Joseph, wise and mild
now don't be cross at this our troupe
it just so happened that we grouped
all here together
birds of a feather
you know, from wood and wild

to greet the sweet Infant Christ Child
we praise him as we're made to do

PIGEONS
a gru hoo a gru hoo
we've come to wrap the Baby round
in a snug and warm eiderdown

FALCONS
a pwee a pwee a pwee a pwee
my brothers, sing with gaiety

ALL THE BIRDS
(whistling singing)

Joseph don't chase us away
that we've come to the Maid to say
what once was a mere prophecy
to us, tonight has come to be
. . . .
thus as the birds their songs intoned
the shutters opened on their own
the lantern showed the Child at rest
asleep in peace on Mary's breast

the Angels flew about in flocks
the donkey the ox the donkey the ox
swayed their huge furry heads in time
to the birds as they chirped and chimed

gaily the birds sang fluttered and flew
while wood and hill bowed in homage too
before the humble crèche
where slept the Word made flesh.

(1920)

AT THE MANGER
(A MYSTERY PLAY)

Tiurli, tiurli — tiurli, tiurli
so the music plays
so the music plays
there, in the shacks
where hemp and flax
and wheat are piled
close by the Child
poor little thing, where He
lies, kneels praying mother Mary
and Joseph too kneels, who also keeps
watch while little Jesus sleeps
on straw, while little Jesus sleeps
. . . .
there by the manger
from the grange are
peasants crowded whispering
the Baby what a bonny thing
He be His little legs His little hands
a pretty lad, so sweet so grand
. . . .
then Kuba came a-squeezing by
and Wicek snags him on the fly
by his sheepskin coat's fleeced hem
he jokes and winks and says Well then
a pretty lad hey? Sweet and grand
(he's right)

KUBA
you're right you clown unhand
my coat you drunk you useless thing
and shut your gob stop jabbering
that Baby is a bonny thing
a pretty lad, so sweet so grand
to greet His birth what did you bring
what present, hey? What did you bring

WICEK
ah Kuba ah you Bachleda
always stuck up and la-di-da
shut your own gob, stop jabbering
to greet His birth what did you bring
what present, hey? What did you bring

KUBA
some cheese some rarebit and a few
other things — gruel, and butter from our ewe
to slake His thirst if He should need
I've brought a little keg of mead

WICEK
ah you Kuba always boasting
drunken useless I'm-the-mosting
stop your bragging
stop your bragging
look you here — I've not been lagging
eh you Kuba of Opiela
don't be such a boasting fella
I've brought Him a turtle dove
a goldfinch chick I know He'll love
two little finches pretty wenches
such as make the forests ring
with song when they've a mind to sing

BACA
hey there sweetlings hey my boys
stop quarrelling stop making noise
be nice shake hands don't grimace smile
look — see? you've woken up the Child
and now He wails and now He shouts
He's kicked apart His swaddling clouts

. . . .
such things the anxious shepherd said
(Meanwhile, everyone looks in dread
toward the door — a wolf's drawn close

well known for strangling sheep by those
who'd rather keep them from his pack

WOLF (with a ram slung on his back)
dear Lord Jesus dear Lord Jesus
pardon me (if so it pleases
You) that I'm a wolf. Here — see?
I kneel in all humility
before your crèche and here set down
the prize I've won from prowling round
from fold to fold from town to town
hau hau! (He sets down on the ground
the ram he'd lugged here from afar)

RAM
Baa, baa, baa
from two folds afar
he's carried me
he's harried me
he's pawed
and clawed
me horridly
baa — baa
(when the Christ Child saw
the animals, from where He's resting
He raised His little hand in blessing)
. . . .
(meanwhile the shepherds pale with fear
huzzahed and chased the wolf from here)

SHEPHERDS
be gone, wild dog, be gone, away
out in the fields you Mongol grey
begone off! off! to the Slovaks!
and nevermore retrace your tracks!
. . . .
(the wolf is gone
and now it's calm

again and bright
in the dark night
shines forth a star
high from afar
so high aloft
above the croft

. . . .

SHEPHERDS (chorus)
see brothers see
above the lea
ah what a light
makes bright the night
the heavens afire
Bethlem afire

. . . .

and now look — here they ride
in caravans from Podola side
crowds and scores
of camels, Moors
and slaves and flunkeys
parrots and monkeys
three kings
and each one brings
gold and myrrh and incense
they're bowing
kow-towing

. . . .

while the music tiurli tiurli
plays the music plays
and in the manger on the hay
the Christ Child sleeps securely
the Christ Child sleeps securely

(1922)

Carolling in the Gigantic City

in the gigantic city people run
in the gigantic city
in the gigantic city flowers dance
in the gigantic city
hej kolęda kolęda
in the gigantic city Christmas Eve
in the gigantic city
in the gigantic city
the bells are chuckling
in the gigantic city
hej kolęda kolęda
in the gigantic city
children are squealing
in the gigantic city
in the gigantic city Christmas trees

- - - - - - - - - - - - - - - - - -

in the gigantic city there's a feast
herring and soup
in the gigantic city

- - - - - - - - - - - - - - - - - -

in the gigantic city misery reels
with dogs snapping at its heels
in the gigantic city
in the gigantic city
hej kolęda kolęda
in the gigantic city shopwindows
in the gigantic city
stand Christmas trees and toys in rows
in the gigantic city through the tall
windows a crib is seen, inside a doll
hej kolęda kolęda
through the gigantic city's wide byways
through the gigantic city
speed on with tinkling bells the horse-drawn sleighs
hey kolęda kolęda
in the gigantic city singing hymns
in the gigantic city

choirs sing about the seraphim
in the gigantic city
in the gigantic city just for fun
in the gigantic city
hej kolęda kolęda
the organist upon his organ thrums
hej kolęda kolęda
everybody to the manger run
hej kolęda kolęda
to greet the Virgin Mary and her Son
hej kolęda kolęda
bring all your instruments with you
hej kolęda kolęda
and don't forget greet Joseph too
in the gigantic city

(1922)

Carols at the Manger
(a mystery play)

What you'll now see once happened when
the word went out from Bethlehem
(a mean and meagre little town)
that Joseph the poor joiner bade
guests come to greet Mary his Maid
who'd given birth in manger cold
to her Child but a few hours old
and all the people came indeed
his brothers friends the Child to greet
they gathered round the crib and sighed
in awe at the fair Babe inside
they all were poor Joseph had less
than most he'd nothing to impress
them with no gold to flash around
no robes no beds no eiderdown
no cradle for the Babe at all
Who naked lay upon the straw

that's where they laid Him down to sleep
and that's where Joseph watch did keep
until the sun long fled away
returned at dawn to bring the day
and flooding all the barn with gold
began to nudge away the cold
then from the sky gyre after gyre
swept down the archangelic choir
like silver doves in deep descents
to do the Child obeisance

GABRIEL (with wings of gold)
Mary worn out with your waking
go now and your rest be taking
for I will rock and lullaby
the Child and calm him should he cry

MICHAEL (he of silver wings)
O my Lady if you need
a tonic now, I'll send for mead
from Heaven's larder with all speed
or whatever else you need

SERAPH (whose wings are burning bright)
up there in heaven we've got lutes
and happy choristers to boot
I'll have them come I'll make them play
and all below will soon be gay

CHOIR OF ANGELS (to each other)
before one circuit of the sun
completes let's choose and send someone
to Heaven's pantry thence to bring
some nourishment for Christ the King

(The Seraphim the Angels
the holy Archangels
spread out wide their snowy wings

to spin gold on a niddy noddy
which as it turns fresh breezes sing
to cool the Holy Child's wee body)

JAN THE SMITH (entering)
and so it's come to pass today
that what was promised came to be
and all the shepherd folk in shifts
have run up here all bearing gifts
senior shepherd and apprentice
sorcerers with their momentous
horoscopes and almanacs
all pushing past each others' backs
running racing panting wheezing
bearing gifts — and there's no reason
Jesus won't find my gift pleasing…

(enter SHEPHERDS — in Chorus)
they told us in the vale below
that Christ the King is reigning now
that our sweet Saviour has been born
for to redeem the world forlorn
hey there fellow have you seen
the little Child the Virgin Queen
and old Joseph the carpenter

JAN THE SMITH
yes my sweet friends here for sure
you've come to the right place the crèche
where God lies taken on our flesh
where Mary kneels and Joseph too

CHORUS OF SHEPHERDS
hey there Joseph stout and true
we've brought some gifts for all of you
whatever each one chanced to find
among his household or his kine

JOSEPH (to Shepherds)
O my sweet and merry friends
thanks for your words may God extend
His blessings on you for coming here
the Holy Child to praise and cheer

BACA ONUFRY
wolves have chased us here today
from Chochołów Vale all the way
running with gifts in sack and punnet
the best he could — each went and done it

BACA FLORIAN
Tomek's ram by wolves was torn
away they only left the horns

BACA ONUFRY
Almighty God that was a fight
Walek was nearly flayed tonight

WALEK
that traitor chased me east and west
through snow and cross the Dunajec
I lost a kierpec in the snow
and nearly froze off my big toe

SHEPHERDS
ha, ha, ha, ha, ha, ha

* * *

the people have such great delight
singing and dancing through the night
the kobzas hum the music rings
the angels sing
and whoosh their wings
while from the east a star sails close
through heaven rolling like a rose

and slowly following
come the Three Magi — kings
from eastern satrapies
arriving they fall to their knees
before the manger of the Lord

CASPAR
O King of all kings Whom the word
of prophets promised long ago
desired of all
for this reason we from afar
set out to follow here the star
before you now prostrate to fall

MELCHIOR
through mountain forest desert clime
we've come to mark the holy time
when God as promised is incarnate
accept us Lord humbly prostrate

BALTHAZAR
our gifts good Lord accept as well
crystal and gold silver vessels
puppets and playthings other presents
and gold and myrrh and frankincense

CHOIR OF ANGELS
Almighty God in mercy send
peace upon earth to all good men

* * *

the music rang the shepherds danced
the Child slept on with folded hands
Mary kept watch in that poor barn
where ox and ass kept Jesus warm

(1923)

Carols at the Crèche
(a mystery play)

PROLOGUE 1
The little sun still hasn't set
the little moon is risen
from wood and mountain music
and shouts of a happy kulig
from field and glade loudly echo
from rattling shutter and window
where frosty designs
in florid lines
with golden weft
suddenly grow bright
like dim embers when breath
stokes them and they ignite
to blaze with light

to Bethlehem they went
a happy mob content
a flock unpent
from vale to vale
from field to field they go
covered in snow
past fir and beechwood juniper
past reed and aster and alder
over freshet
and over stream they went
the dark clouds frowned
the woods went brown
while stars up high
and huts near by
grew pale and calm
awaiting the dawn

BASSES
hudu – hudu – hu
mayu – grayu – u

dear Lord Jesus true
God-Man we play for You

FIDDLES
tiri, tiri, tili, tili
plain on fiddles play on gaily
veelee – lee – veelee – vee
from the dawn until the eve

KOBZA
meh – eh – leh – meh –
billy – beh – billy – meh
half-a-groat my billy goat

CLARINET
mula – ula u la la
mama mama matulina
in a lean-to for to screen her
from all danger in the manger
keep the Baby safe from danger
u – la – la

BASSES
Lord for You
one God and true
Man we play we do

CLARINET
screen her screen her
matulina
leb koleba kolebina

FIDDLES
veelee – vee – veelee – vee
from the dawn unto the eve

BASSES
Lord God True
Man-God to You we play we do

PROLOGUE 2
the shepherds meanwhile
came to seek the Christ Child
the fiddlers stopped sawing
the sheep began baaing
and then the manger stood revealed
high in the Tatras on Szumska field

THE MANGER

SHEPHERDS
down in the dales where it's black night
we've waited on this blessed sight
of Jesus the Lord God's true Son
born in the manger before dawn
slip off your kierpce boys so we
might enter with propriety

ORGANIST
O God's people brothers come
here to the manger on the run
you seek the hidden God? come see
here in the manger — it is He

WALEK
I searched the barn and the grain-bin
but found no one nor kith nor kin

ONUFRY
I've searched the cliffs and the couloirs
where is He hid this Babe of ours?

JEW
gentlemen shepherds why this scurry
why are you frowning why do you worry
ask and you shall receive
a Jew once said now best believe
just go to Nowy Sącz and there
you'll find the Virgin in the square
with the Child safe in her arms

GYPSY
kaciary-maciary now I heard swarms
of folk in Witów say that He
is in the palace go and see
that's what I heard upon my life
you don't trust me? go ask my wife

ŁAPAJ THE DOG
hau-hau, hau
I know that gypsy — him I know
don't you believe what he should say
the Child is here safe in the hay

CHORUS OF SHEPHERDS
is it dusk or is it dawning
all the universe alight
golden sparks are flaming bright
by the rooftree by the awning
in the manger and the straw
they glow upon both ridge and brow
of cliff in manger in the hay
where all together grouping they
stand — the most Holy Family
Jesus Joseph and Mary
now see the angels swooping low
like thickly falling flakes of snow
silver white the angels winging
playing golden zithers singing

SHEPHERDS
little goats and woolly rams
ducks and mallards little lambs
barrels four of mead sweet and clear
some moonshine and a case of beer
and honeybees from hive a-buzzing
and strings of ram-gut a full dozen
we bring as gifts unto the Lord

OX
who would not warm Him with his breath
shepherds? so cold he'd freeze to death

ASS
who would not jump and skip about
my tail is froze it's so cold out

SHEPHERDS
hush now hush and genuflect
pay the Child Jesus meet respect
and you musicians lay it on
play from the dusk until it's dawn
and we'll sing for God's only son

ORGANIST
no more music no more singing
look here what the star is bringing
frankincense and gold and fleece
pouncet-boxes, fripperies
and jewels feathers purple dyes
such things they bring these three kings wise
all to lay before the Lord
Balthazar Caspar Melchior

CHORUS OF SHEPHERDS
there's kings for you now if you please
golden pomp, gold liveries
their servants put on golden airs

their carts are gold, stallions and mares
scimitared guards protect their sires
and blackamoors mix with the squires

BALTHAZAR
Balthazar I a famous king
to you Lord of all lords I bring
obeisance and wonders rare
along with servants and fanfare

MELCHIOR
Melchior I an eastern king
from Eden's garden bounds I bring
grapes and dates and delicacies
a cask of gold full and its keys

CASPAR
the star led us across the seas
the sun would scorch the snows would freeze
but as cool wells in deserts glow
so these pearls which I give to You now

SHEPHERDS
the worlds they turn and spin aloft
the birds are chirping in the croft
the little Child sleeps on the hay
'twixt the old joiner and the Maid
and like woodpeckers in the oak
in swarms flit near angelic folk
so let us play and let us sing
setting our basses muttering
just like the finches in the clearing
hosa – holasa, hosa – holasa
softly the music softly cheering

EPILOGUE
and so they came and so they stayed
shepherds and kings with Child and Maid

the stars the cliffs and all the beasts
before God's manger on their knees
and sun and moon up in the sky
shone down upon them from on high

(1924)

Robespierre. Rhapsody. Cinema.

From Romanticism to Cynicism.

(1927)

Robespierre
A poem

The faded silken pennants remained — the earth slipped, and man rumbled down like a barrel of wine.
This is nothing more than the poem of parting leaves, racing in the fall, to arrive at their finish line and sink into a red pond.
Above a depth of black marble there spurts the whiteness of a pregnant Nymph, the organs are shattered, in the church they creak like old type on a printer's board.
Flowers re-enter the burnt wood, in decrepit graves the bones weep with rot, or become one with the earth and grow into wildflowers

And the earth yearns to return to the sun
Reevaluating the earth, the sun wishes to make her
rounder at the poles carved from a cube of white marble,
All the marble in monuments, knights, nymphs,
Kings, satyrs, dianas, madonnas, venuses
And saints yearns to return to the earth
And then, like a swallow to her nest, poetry flew up
But then again she was the dove from Noah's ark
Noah, father of the young earth, whose dove flutters to the trees in blossom
to the blades of the flowers
Or the future trees
Green trees
In the forests oaken chaplets wound with roses and lilies of the valley and rose leaves

And leaves of the spreading oak,
These are neither lilies of the valley nor roses nor autumn asters
Nor oak leaves but a swarm of people who pass in the street who flood
over the roofs of buildings
to the very horizon where the river of grey clouds bursts in foam against
the walls

Freedom, how beautiful the word and how mutable like the colour of
the sky in fall
The yellow autumn acacias toss into the city as if into a letterbox their
pale ochre leaves
which dry in the sun
Large graves have been dug, common graves in the cemeteries and
meanwhile withered leaves fall there and the wind whirls the dust of
the earth into dancing columns. It is both gay and sad.
Man is a house through the chambers of which the heart paces, man is
vile
Robespierre paced by. I saw him, his face was bloodless his blood had
flowed down into his hands, his fingers. He had a heart full of blood
the Face of Robespierre was the stomach of a vomiting child who sobs
and fears
if I speak of Robespierre I wish to see him when he rests his hands upon
his bosom like supple reeds, while before his brow his eyes go misty, an
autumn evening in the swarming streets, setting his feet firmly upon
the earth a church from the façade of which the heads of granite saints
have been lopped
And those saints
Are letters snipped from scriptures and tossed onto the ground like
rubbish
There is no God he is not here
He left his office or maybe a crowd of people murdered him in a narrow
street on the corner,
at the very foot of his own porch?
He runs off
If I catch sight of Robespierre sneaking out of his house, he has pulled
on his tail-coat and runs off to the Council of the Convention
To murder, to gather the red apples ripe of the trees to cut to slice
the Pomegranate so that its sweet, sticky juice might flow.

God and Robespierre these two gaze at one another like friends these two have long known one another, which of them knows his own strength? God spreads wide his legs his hand, each finger as stiff as a column, setting them one by one upon the wall.
Robespierre gazes at the ground, draws, gouges and digs in search of the seeds sown by God.

Robespierre sees the brain which is the lord of the people, and remembers that, back home, he fell in love at first with sparrows and pigeons. He runs off into the rags of streets and writhes like a worm
a good worm, an irritated scorpion and he wounds dogs, teases cats with dogs, gives himself over to onanism in lonely and mouldy lavatories,
He was no different from the others
He gave his first lover a wreath of roses and at night on their bed of love they tore it apart in play, petal by petal, petal by petal creating billows of letters white and red:
The Nation which roiled in yearning for a larger, newer hive.
Cold surrender and reasonable frenzy.
Nation and Freedom and a word slimy with pus like a wound
Revolution.
Like frozen iron numbers, in bank accounts, like expressions upon waking
he ought he has
Or as Jean-Jaques Rousseau puts it: 'Protect the heart against evil, the mind against error, and live satisfied, happy and free, as nature lives herself.'

If the teeth should rattle like the gate of the head from the chill or before lovemaking, when I am relaxed from my last sexual encounter... The same with that word Freedom.
If I should desire the death of my enemies.
If I should bark to the crowd, search with my eyes which like to serve and humble themselves.

DANTON
Citizen patriots. A great storm has humbled a Nation of tyrants. Evil is vanquished. The Revolution and the People demand their rights. The traitors cringe in basements hiding like rats

It's not me

Death death
Murder! like someone playing with fire pissing on the flames. When they're burning rubbish on the boulevards
Ah, what joy as the smoke and flames fly
With the wind
Ah what delight when the blood drips
Through the narrow bottleneck
And the wind flutters the booming voice of howling drums and the banners are pulled tight
The blood spurts
Where is Robespierre my friend
Here
Freedom has no tyrants, to the knife
The florist in the street places leaf to leaf and offers for sale bouquets of lilies of the valley.
From among the lilies of the valley there emerges a head with eyes of the setting sun and wet lips. The people intone the litany and place the silk ribbon of razor to his throat
A gun booms
The bullet is fixed in the host, a rain of gold sifts down upon the whiteness of the cloth
Miracle, miracle there are no miracles
There is a glacier — the tongue of the orator and the red glow of the burning mind above the city

ROBESPIERRE
I left home I was a calm sheep in the flock
Citizen people I thrust the knife into the heart

GOD

And the heart is an omnibus that rumbles through the gate of St Dominic.

To arms

Let the legs shatter against the cobblestones and let them spread their arms crosswise like withered trees.
We shall use the wood of the cross to make a guillotine
Cannons were placed at Port Royal gaily bedecked in oak leaves they crouch down like lions drunk on wine and yawn in the direction of the city
The bell sounds to arms and within the people bones begin to crunch whilst above the city blossoms the shaggy pall of smoke. Music sounds in the streets and people dance and a band in carnival masks pries open the bakery doors
Hunting for bread
Aromatic fresh bread, joyful days and bright green mornings in the gentle marbled courtyards of palaces where fountains chat amongst themselves in rainbows of water
The tame Naiads revel

In the mirrored library chests of books that sleep that dream their contents and romances with the king
In the square before Saint-Sulpice the Republican Guard has made an arrest on the basis of a denunciation.
It was God. Led into the commissariat he was found to have no papers

ROBESPIERRE
Who are you?

GOD
God.

ROBESPIERRE
An aristocrat!

GOD
In and of myself.

ROBESPIERRE
Why did you go out into the city, whereas you well know that it is forbidden to tread upon liberty
Why do you tread upon her with your sandals of God. Why do you give ear to the words of your priests, who are black flags upon your head. Why do you want to kill liberty?!

GOD
Why do you slice the apples that I have hung upon the trees
Why do you tear apart the silken grape, whereas the seeds are not yet formed Why do you have my wine poured out into the street gutters, my wine which you call blood.
Why do you drill a heated iron rod into brains, while the brain sprawls wide like a woman about to give birth?

ROBESPIERRE
Why do you command me to die Why do you shove a hungry dog in front of the church so that he might sniff out who enters and who exits?
Why did you *give* the beggar rags and a hunchback with which he goes to your mass
You have sown nettles and rye — the rye you soaked in water and showed to the rats, playing at this like a little child playing
You have directed kings and bishops to stand before the altar wash the wine from their hands and blossom like peonies

GOD
Why do you not say that I hold not only intelligence in my palm, but the heart as well?!

ROBESPIERRE
You have led satin mares before the bronze-spiralled stallions of human thought and you call that love, which is lust or glory or the poetry of weakness.

GOD
You adorn yourself with the love of woman merely ambushing her knees.

ROBESPIERRE
Am I a shrinking fox Do I flee destiny?

GOD
You wish to plunder and fell the trees — and you are unable to locate the seed that sleeps in the depths of the rock, hidden from your lenses.

ROBESPIERRE
So tell me what shall become of your intelligence with which you have constructed the seed?

GOD
So tell me what will become of your intelligence when you bind your head with a wet, red rag and wish to proceed further?

ROBESPIERRE
Do you kill the body so that roses might sprout from the flesh?

GOD
Do you pluck roses so as to toss them upon copses?

ROBESPIERRE
Amongst the roses you have sown cynicism.

GOD
And you have bound a bouquet of roses, and cynicism.

ROBESPIERRE
And this is why I toss that bouquet upon corpses.

GOD
I have possessed you with a mania, which you have taken for the idea of liberty.

ROBESPIERRE
I have discharged my carbine and the bullet has flown too far — and now you want it to retrace its flight.

GOD
You were my bullet, and so I take you once more in my fingers.

ROBESPIERRE
I have struck with the will and you still go on about destiny.

GOD
Choose.

ROBESPIERRE
I have chosen.

The meadows beyond the houses have already covered themselves with green and the sun has arisen like a gigantic block of ice that melts above the city
dripping heavy sparkling drops.
It was a beautiful and innocent day when the sun arose, clinging to the sky with a thousand rays like a spider.
The joiners are splitting beams on the Place de la Revolution,
and their axes flash like wandering stars
thumping into the wood like
a swarm of bees two feet away
Robespierre's face is pale, the fingers of his right hand bristle like the thorns of the crown on Christ's head when he was hanging upon the cross
And the crowd runs along the street with music, on their lapels they wear revolutionary cockades and flowers and the joy of beggars and it's the holiday of street girls, the holiday of the unsatisfied, of the hungry and ragged and dirty and lousy,
all of the street corners have blossomed like gardens
the colours of which have been destroyed by the sun
and the colours that the sun has extracted grow bright and bloom.

ROBESPIERRE
Build the guillotine, beam to beam, brace to brace, clamp to clamp, construct the parquet of the scaffold like a ballroom

JOINER
This work is as hard as sadness — our sweat flows in the heat like rain in the mountains

ROBESPIERRE
Work on, it is the world's largest throne that you are building

JOINER
Will it reach the heavens?

ROBESPIERRE
It will surpass the clouds and reach the stars, straight of plumb and slender as
Diana
Let God catch sight of it and let him gaze upon it.

And so they work from morning until black evening
And one can hear the measured snap of the knife
And the blade grows dull like that of a scythe on mountain slopes

Two friends are talking:

DANTON
You have given me over to death, wishing to learn if my heart has shot into my mind, or were you jealous of my heart which turned at high tide and low like the sea.

ROBESPIERRE
You paused for thought in the middle of your road and meditated, is death your friend or your enemy.

DANTON
Understand this, that not only death is the lord of the city, but that there are also beings who love one another…

CONTRESCARPE

There is a little house on the rue Contrescarpe a jolly little house, asleep. Cats drowse in the sun near the gate like little cotton lions. In front of the house, the wife of the concierge pierces a stocking with shining needles. Her fat cheeks are lit up by the sun and the tufts of her black hair are like cypress boughs when the wind rocks them.
From the farthest narrowing of the street, from the dark drawer of his office, comes a man in a blue tail-coat.

ROBESPIERRE
Does Catherine Théot live here, the mother of God?!

CONCIERGE'S WIFE
Madame Théot lives here, but no mother of God.

At the end of the corridor lies a dark chamber where humidity ambles from corner to corner like the wind, scrambles up the chimney to the sky and returns through door and window, agitating the faded drapes, rustling the pages of books, while in the quiet one hears the bells chime the hours, all of the bells in the steeples of Ste. Geneviève, Saint-Séverin, Saint-Eustache and Notre Dame. They mark the passing time of: life, love, and death.

CATHERINE THÉOT

I shall read the words of the books of Ezekiel
hear now what I say unto you, I mother of the new
God:
And the thrones shall tumble from the heights of their towers
and there shall appear a man
as sharp as the blade of a sword who
shall shave the hairs from the overgrown chin.
The heads of kings and tyrants shall fall
and roll along like swollen overripe pumpkins,
and the greatest man-beast shall arise

and the beasts shall arise: lions, panthers, monkeys with the tongues of
man, hippocentaurs,
fish like submarine boats, lilies passing over the earth, rocks
with winking human eyes,
and the people shall grow and grow — like ears of corn on a gigantic field
They shall extend their spring-motion arms to the copses, to the forests,
to the seas
of busty waves
and to the free burning steppe.
Silence is the most beautiful music because
it is the mother of the poor, drops of rain
that slide down the bark of trees, and long
drawn out threads of the voice of the flute,
is there no good answer to misery
to the desire to live,
But then shall arise a man who shall be
a Skull-God
for people and he shall construct
his throne of his own intelligence.

ROBESPIERRE
The weather is fine and the shadows of the trees
at dusk are like my thoughts of good and evil
good is the earth lit up by the sun,
shadows are evil.

MOTHER OF GOD
When the sun slowly slides
as if dancing
the clock of God moves over the sky, like a burning hand and shadows
change the appearance of things on earth.

ROBESPIERRE
When I stand in the sun I cast a shadow
my shadow walks upon the earth, like me alive
when my heart rustles within me like an anthill
the great Anthill which is inside your heart —

broaden the streets, extend the roads, spread wide the earth like an umbrella.
To arms, to arms, there is no time to talk to oneself.
Purify the brain open it as one undoes the safety of a gun.

A NON-IDYLLIC LOVE

Pleasant summer days in the countryside, people are working in the fields, their sickles flashing.
Forget-me-nots are blooming above the pond; the sky gazes at them, and love hides in them, like an echo in the woods.
When one speaks of love, walking step by step into the fields beyond the city. A bird is a singer that squeezes into the copula of the heavens and sings every quarter hour, every half hour, every hour.
A singing bird — a clock in the field, and bared
breasts with rosy, tight nipples
At night darkness embraces everything like black cloth tacked to the city.
At night each embrace is a mountain or a wave of the sea. What is love?

From confession to triumph. Night, city, the desire to drowse and hands searching for hips and breasts, the voice is dammed up in the chest like a river is dammed at a water gate, the breath whistles in the throat and flies out between the teeth like a cyclone.
To touch delight, to be weak for a moment and then to awaken strong triumphant.

SHE
The death of my body is the same thing as a sigh.
As I was walking through the Place du Carrousel one spring day: flowers and tulips and hyacinths.
As I walked I thought about the ambition and the endurance of the will of Robespierre. The People of Paris were saying: This all must come to an end, liberty has surpassed liberty, after one freedom comes another freedom, after one desire comes another desire, a constant chase, from misery to death, from the illusion of happiness to happiness.

ROBESPIERRE
Happiness is not found in this, that you or I are happy; rather, happiness is this: that we long for happiness and purify ourselves through the crimes of the revolution.

SHE
On whose behalf?

ROBESPIERRE
On behalf of the others who regain possession of a new order of things and desire a new happiness.
Triumph is like the wings of a bird.

THE TRIUMPH OF THE SUPREME BEING

ROBESPIERRE
The triumph of reason.

On a wagon decorated with poppies of the field, above an *allegory* of happiness, stands a naked, pregnant woman. The People approach and do her homage.
Bells and cannons converse like brothers and sisters. This is the holiday of the Supreme Being, the holiday of love, equality, parental love, sisterly and fraternal love, the love of nature, Stoicism, Reason, good will, the holiday of kisses, copulation, Delight, shadow and light.

ROBESPIERRE
I have lain the torch to the pyre, flames gnaw at the statue of Obscurantism and Falsehood, and from this moment I believe that I shall surmount past God like the smoke rising; I shall break through myself and all others.

THE TRIBUNAL

The hall of the Convention is filled with people. The galleries and loges and balconies are full of curious onlookers waiting upon the battle that will be played out before them, concerning them. There are two paths: to stop and retreat, or: to go on further. There are two rivers — one flowing slowly, majestically, through city and field, the blue ribbon of France. The other river, more passionate, with water so dark it looks as if it were to flow into the Styx, bears along its current foreign desires and forgetfulness. There are other rivers too: the Seine and the Marne and the green Rhône flowing over its stones toward forests of eucalyptus and copses of mimosa. The violet-blue Loire slipping like a snake between ancient castles and palaces. The hall is filled to bursting and hatred, envy and vengeance wheel through the air like gulls. Robespierre thinks: I have choked upon the thoughts of others enough, already; they have latched onto me like river leeches onto the legs of horses. The People are either silent or they howl like a hungry dog. Always thirsting for blood. And so today there is a rosary of deeds and a rosary of heads threaded upon a cord of silk, and these I pass quickly through my great swollen fingers.

JUDGE
Respond!

ROBESPIERRE
I always held my hand upon my heart. My enemies thought that I was looking for a source from which to suck strength.

JUDGE
You have been charged with treason: against the people, treason against humanity, hatred of Love, the supremacy of reason, of soaring lonely ambition, you wished to be God…hein?!

MOB
To the knife with the tyrant! Death!

JUDGE
Your friend Saint-Just, your Jacobin friends, your younger brother — let them defend you, ha ha… You pushed your way above the crowd, now be levelled with the crowd again. Another *I* is mightier than your bloody *I*!

ROBESPIERRE
I…

MOB
Death, death!!

JUDGE
You spoilt, you whipped up the people to crime, you set fire to the house of the Republic and the terror of death slithers among the people!

ROBESPIERRE
I did not look beyond or around me, I did not rummage through my conscience as if it were a medical encyclopaedia.
I strode directly towards the triumph of man over…

JUDGE
Now your time has come, now death shall triumph over you.

ROBESPIERRE
I wanted the triumph, the triumph!…

JUDGE
Of hatred?!…

MOB
Death, death!!

ROBESPIERRE'S HEAD

The head is slowly extinguished, and one eye beholds a gigantic white landscape of snow, where one might sweep, glide, borne along by the wind over the white waves of the canvas. Little threads flow from the fresh wound, upon the white landscape of sad snow, which is a shroud of white canvas, rivers which expand from one point, forming a Delta of blood. And from the delta there flow little streams searching for an estuary in the beds of white canvas. Robespierre lay like this and listened.
The trees talked amongst themselves, or, more precisely, their leaves chattered. They talked about how, being on the branches of the trees, they cast shade and took to themselves nests with families of birds. The

leaves were torn from the trees, the limbs were hacked off, and they decorated: cities, houses, and the guillotine.

The spring snapped free the weight of the blade, thoughts surged and swirled and grasped onto any small pebble, any clod of earth, any nail driven into any plank. The head fell and rolled into a great basket lined with leaves — so that the blood should not seep through.

(Paris – Warsaw 1926–1927)

RHAPSODY

I. Over the Bay the Sun

The leaves crawl
and the gums
grow golden like mums
blooms, palms, vines in the red autumn

fish out of water
across the beach scatter
mermaids lure and chatter
pirates rape and flatter.

Stone castles and castellos
vineyards and taverns — infernos
manor timbers moulder
live embers smoulder
coals in bread-ovens glowing
on the fields fire throwing
in waves of green growing
the earth moans: I'm drowning
and the cities in the afternoon, white,
doors agape, screech in delight.

(St. Raphaël 1925)

II. Wings above Cagnes

The screams of white wings — puffs of mist;
Tattered by tears; and curlicues
Of mermaids' voices and submarine
Pink oranges and lemons, breasts
Brown and alpine, cataracts of dews
And voices musical, undone
Like Venus wading toward the gravel
Shingle, conscious tufts of foam

Which like the dawn the seas unravel
Speed to the shore — the sun is setting —
The sun I loved, it wades and roams,
Sailing the sea to lands and days
To stand and puff out waves and sails,
Unlatch the dovecotes, so they might
To trunks and leaves, fly off, to glades.
Sails — droopy squids — uncover bays
Afar — doves, slopes and towns set alight
In red, igniting thought and walls
And Roman columns set up higher
On mountains, gum trees, snows and stoops
On stoops, harps, ribbon-bound scrolls
Graveyard yews, cries of 'vampire'
Bells to cry out their dread and swoop
On feathers to the dales of men,
Ringing at shutters, zithers chime
Discordant concord of gold strings.
Black, red, illusions in fountains
To swell with smoke and shatter shrines
Eritrean, to dress the gods in strings
Of roses, fleece, ivy, with streams
Of waterfalls to gild the depths
With veils of wine, lilac and sloe,
Where Artemis, shod, abed, dreams.
The glades at dawn in glassy dew,
Actaeon's teased unto his death.
In his maw rose and dew he's fretting.
The smoke obscures the dawning sun.
Above the banks, the winged string plays,
The red earth barks, red-tribed thighs,
Winged cloaks, arches, moans and runs,
Black-crimson mirrored infernos blaze;
In the woods fight: gods, birds, men, skies.

III. To the Manes of Juliusz Słowacki

In the nether regions, where their grey shades flit
Covered by the owlish wings of the night,
And the barque of Charon waits to set sail
For the land of oblivion and night,
Of Lethe's liquor having not yet sipped
(And so they still live, in the ravenous might
Of deeds) — such shades as these declaim and wail:
The Nation's Glory and Life, through manhood!
They guard their brothers' freedom, with swords gripped
Tight, holding the keys to the People's Synod,
And a black hammer, forged by the folk, of steel,
And sheaves of wheat, which in summer matures,
Handfuls of grain to be sown in the field,
Snakes — supple arches, darts fatally sure,
Caskets of dust and tears (yet these they pass on),
Whetting their swords before the sun should dawn,
They dress in armour to meet the sun's rays
And send their thoughts like envoys crying War.
They stab the earth before God with their knees
And bend their bows to make their arrows soar;
They begged their sacrifice to be offered, now,
That no fear make them tremble like the leaves,
Though Destiny's chalice might overflow,
So that they might temper their wings of steel
On songs eternal, songs of war, the kind
Their people heed from ancient days, and wheel
In battle, and congregate in massy troops,
Brothers in love with death and with hazard,
Taking to them the flagging soul that droops
To stir it with the war songs of their bard,
The vulture. So they went, flags beating the air,
A group of knights, through flower-covered lea,
And groups of hearts all thrumming like a lyre,
And following them, their soldier's destiny;
Both eagles and doves — a chattering flock,
The while to flowers there flew a hive of bees

And after them, the unshod beggars walked.
. . . .
When bugles called them at dawn to the battle
(At dawn, the light of which was golden-hoary)
To bathe in mire and others' blood to spatter,
Their Inspiration was both Song and Glory.
They took their swords into their flaming hands,
Their swords that flashed in sunlight steely-blue;
The breeze blew war-songs over the flowering land,
And on the rock sparked the steed's golden shoe.
. . . .
When the wing-footed song croaks on dead lips,
When all these perish: head and hand and breath,
Above the soldier's corpse sad Vengeance dips
And lets fly: Curse, Inspiration, Glory, Death.
O Mother our Fatherland O Earth
What strength is drowsing in us, your offspring,
To whom, for your defence, you've given birth?
What words, these ghosts inspired are whispering?
. . . .
Where Life and Death and Vengeance is, and Glory,
Where living flesh is torn by teeth and taloned hands,
Where anger and despair, and man with man is warring
And darts are flung by the hand of sightless Chance,
There Nike soars upon archangel's wings
And beautiful, pure thought, whose figure stands
A daring deity, that from forehead springs,
There you went, and were with them — Fatherland…
. . . .
And so their whole day passed in this way, warring,
The bloody sun declining to the west;
Less thirsty they for benefit than glory;
More sacrifice, and victory the less.
The evening came, and down they lay their tired
Limbs and exhausted heads for a night's sleep.
Night came, and sputtered out all the camp fires
While Sleep, with such dreams through their souls did creep:
A flame sprang from the earth and to the sky

Stretched like a monstrous flower. Grand it stood:
And then a great mountain, red, rushed from on high
Into a chasm, a waterfall of blood.
From this Siklawa, a bloody stream now grows
To plummet through a valley populous.
They hold their breaths — their hearts are fairly froze,
And yet they rise! To breast the bloody waves,
To dam the flooding river, locking arms,
From death their fellow-countrymen to save
(Thinking: courage and will avert yet greater harms).
The floodwaves thump their bodies like crowbars,
Cliff-smashing, rushing into the abyss.
But then a voice, louder than storms by far:
'Valorous deeds win too!' Like God's voice it is…
. . . .
Then they arose at the bugled alarms,
For dawn had come — to action the camp stirred.
Thousands of rested hands now gripping arms,
Their nightly fingers like the claws of birds…
. . . .
When one stands face to face with final matters,
The just man chooses the most beautiful;
Just like the squire, when he about him gathers
His men, awarding those proven most faithful,
Thus we, our thoughts and deeds should justly weigh,
The dearest to our soul, the ones our heart
Most loved, about which we can truly say
'These must be saved. These must be set apart.'
. . . .
In the netherworld, where those grey shades flit,
Covered beneath the wings of gloomy night,
Who yet of Lethe's waters have not sipped,
Whose brows with misty musing still are bright,
They hear, as they go into death and dark,
Echoing sevenfold, though it slowly thins,
Like to a distant storm (though louder by far)
Thunderous speech: 'The valorous deed, too, wins'.

IV. A Conversation

ROBESPIERRE
There's only one thing for which I won't stand:
Weeping. I wanted to march into the grave
Lily-wreathed. Should pearly, crunching death stand
Between me, blood, and lily: I am saved.

SPIRIT
Here at the water's edge where we are standing,
Where vermin multiply and make it throb,
Above the scum, here on this bitchy landing,
Repent, repent, and thus escape the mob.

ROBESPIERRE
If 'twas with human blood my pen was full,
If I walked on the edge of a stiletto,
What if I left this earth like to a ghoul
Who has no fear of human skeleton?

SPIRIT
People need skeletons, to stand and walk.
Like truths, which are well-known to every sort.
Since you chose not to be the people's rock,
Why did you quake before the people's court?

ROBESPIERRE
Who on their banners had a death's head sewn,
Sang psalms as well — dirges from charnel house.
They were new truths that I held for my own.
I fear lest, with my blood, they shall run out.

SPIRIT
Digging in heels against fate, so you stood,
Then went on, further, further than right here
Where the Host's broken, where water becomes blood —
You fought with death, all to arrive, well, where?

ROBESPIERRE
I fought with death and toasted her with gore.
I set my signature to freedom's acts.
Corpse-like, unlilting, a cold knife I bore;
I sprang from earth; the garden takes me back.

SPIRIT
The frock you wear, against death you once dragged,
Befouling in stench the amaranthine cloak.
Along the way you lost love, just like a bag
That God gave you one day as the dawn broke.

ROBESPIERRE
I passed through padlocks and walls of the grave.
The earth, its laws, the people's truths I broke;
Destroying ancient truths, new truths I gave,
And above God Himself I soared like smoke.

SPIRIT
The truth is one, ever the same, and whole.
The tree rises from rot and wilted grass,
And though the sun's disk ever more shall roll,
Nor you, nor it, beyond death's reach shall pass.

(Cagne sur mer, Paris, 1925–1926)

Cinema

On squalid tattered trousers
that rag, that banner of failed revolution
on faces spat upon, on hands scorched
by the glowing coals of a stove
a certain whore gazed, from past the corner
of a white house in Warsaw.
So the rats emerged from the sewers
young girls emerged from the churches
nuns emerged from the cloisters
and a crowd of cars from courts up-lurches
to the cinematic churches.

          CINEMATIC PRESENTATION
            I: "The Drama of the Fallen"
      II: "The Noble Heart, or Teeth Fallen Out"

A certain wife of a certain man
determined to abuse the sacrament
a letter she composed and said: amen
to test the manliness of her man
and life laughed aloud curled into a ball
behind the paravane the patterned screen
a monkey laughed aloud, and Buddha too.
The butler was a hypocrite, a liar
as was also the masseuse-for-hire.
There was a pistol, just in case
like a pocket guillotine.
And thus began the final scene.
An advert blinked above the cinema,
the husband made peace with his pa-in-law,
the drama finished WC-ly,
the lady dying — nobly, seemly.

From Romanticism to Cynicism

I had no political, historical, or historiosophical intention in composing my *Robespierre* and *Rhapsody*. I offer nothing in them but poetry, constructed according to artistic laws such as I consider to be most appropriate, issuing forth from my being, my poetic organism. Through my constructions of poetic form I wish to rescue poetry from the jaws of death. For poetry, unfortunately, in recent times, and at the hands of people with no vocation thereto, has become piece-work 'more convenable to shoemakers than Apollo'. I endow each word that appears in my poetry with individual significance and autonomy; at the same time, via the anarchisation (not anarchy) of words, I separate them into groups of analogous words, from which I elicit analogous phrases, etc. For this reason, words and phrases, despite a frequently superficial alogicality, as a whole (through the contrast of bonding materials) result in a cohesive entity, which lives like an organism in the natural world. Now, I don't wish to identify my works with the works of nature — by giving them their own life and autonomy, in this way I protect them from the literary levelling from which contemporary poetic works suffer. The written or spoken word, regardless of its consequent relationship to the phrase, or the so-called sense, is a living entity, which affords the possibility of life to the suggestive idea with which it is imbued. To offer some similar, earlier experiments of mine as examples, I would point to a few of the longer poems in *The Green Eye* (1920) and *Electric Visions* (1919), as well as a few of my *Pastorals* (Paris, 1925) — which some have mistakenly — and quite unjustly — considered popular/folkloristic pastiches. My relationship to the most recent Polish poetry is both close, and at the same time very distant. Having belonged at one time to the Kraków Group of so-called Futurists and Formists — to which the poets Bruno Jasieński and Stanisław Młodożeniec also belonged — I was, along with them, one of the creators of that poetic movement in Poland, which exerted the greatest influence upon the younger poets, as well as upon a few older poets of the period of 'Young Poland' symbolism — which was drawing to a close. It is nevertheless strange that, today, neither the youngest poets, nor those of the older generation, will admit to this, but rather ignore my poetic works, and those of my colleagues. Once (around the year 1920), I was cried up as the 'poet of the machine' on account of my volume of poems entitled *Night and Day* (1922). In the artistic periodical that I was bringing out at the time in Kraków, beginning in 1919, I underscored the existence of the machine as one of the characteristic forms of contemporary life. However, I never set up the machine as some sort of absolute poetic 'object' or any *signum temporis* of a contemporary world-view. It was Mr Tadeusz Peiper who did this, subsequently, in his periodical *The Switch*, where he published the article 'City, Mass, Machine.' I collaborated in a few issues of *The Switch* until my departure from the country for an extended period of time, at which my ties with both the country and the periodical were severed. I am absolutely opposed to the abuse and manneristic misuse of 'machinism' in poetry, as professed by Mr Peiper and those colleagues of his, congregated around the present-day *Switch*. After I myself, Jasieński, and Młodożeniec ceased to collaborate with that group, Poetry took fright at continually being smeared with the odourless grease of machines, and fled *The Switch*. Even the verses of Mr Tadeusz Peiper himself (despite his even considerable phraseological and rhetorical abilities, as these are currently understood), could not restrain her flight. From that time on, our existence was considered null and void by the editorial board of *The Switch*, and neither my *Pastorals* (which were later published), nor Młodożeniec's *Squares* nor Jasieński's *A Word on Jakub Szela* made an echo there, or received even the briefest mention. Long live Cliqueomania! Here we have one more contribution to the history of stubborn fury in Polish literature. Nonetheless, this did not prevent many of the 'youngest' poets of both sexes from appropriating our achievements and our poetic material 'with gusto.' Today, the very same people who wrung their hands in anguish over the 'disfiguration of poetry' that they found in our 'one day ephemeral' *Nife in the Stummik* are writing lengthy narrative poems about machines, 'primitive' madonnas, aeroplanes and the Dynamo. But such is the usual course of events. Unfortunately, criticism in Poland does not exist — certainly no sort of criticism that understands and is favourably inclined to the youngest art and poetry. In Poland, ethics and plain-dealing in questions of criticism and the evaluation of art have disappeared. 'Be a nice boy now, sit still, don't outgrow the others by too much, and maybe we'll write something about you.' Such, we see, is the very personal motto of the contemporary critic. The baseless antipathy (or rather the well-founded envy); the malicious, scornful neglect of both my poetry and my painting; the constant deafening critical silence concerning great poets like Bruno Jasieński and Stanisław Młodożeniec provides one with much food for thought. On the one hand, having enemies amongst a certain group of poets who have overexploited and exhausted their Rimbaudian poetics, but continue to lead their poetic life, writing cloying 'madrigals' — and on the other, being attacked by a certain group of the youngest poets who are *plus papistes que le pape*, who without too profound a consideration or experience of their art — as they are not gifted with excessive creative powers — compose nonsense and, unfortunately, bring it out in print — I and my colleagues find ourselves between the rock and the hard place of perfidy and intolerance. That funny little tag — the term 'futurist' — with which they continually categorise us — is proof positive of their lack of a desire to comprehend our work. The term 'formism' has been abused, and the meaning of that movement diminished and twisted. At the moment, I do not wish to dilate upon this theme, to which I will return in the book I am currently writing, which will be, like Verlaine's *Les poëtes maudits*, a settling of accounts with and synthesis of the most recent poetry and art in Poland. But here I must emphasise (I don't know if it be the injustice or the insouciance) of certain critics. For example: I have been overlooked and neglected by Prof. Szyjkowski in his sketch of the youngest generation of Polish poets (published abroad in Vienna) — I have been passed over by Mr Lorentowicz — just as Jasieński and Młodożeniec were — in one of his articles in *The World* entitled 'On the Most Recent Polish Poetry.' Many other examples might be given, but I don't want to list all the names. Anyway, the names don't change, but the character and the cliques do. Prof. Szyjkowski has forgotten that he once wrote paeans to us in an article of his published in the *Illustrated Daily Courier* in Kraków, in the style of 'Poetry of Storm and Stress,' etc., or, what is more, that he himself initiated the production of my futuristic play *Donkey and Sun in Metamorphosis*, which was staged by the artists of the Bagatela Theatre. The most 'meritoriously' windy of critics, Mr Irzykowski, who at one time did battle with us, armed to the teeth with all his assets of incomprehension, succumbed to the illusion that he 'cleared the field,' indeed scorching the earth (and in so doing creating a nice advertisement for us on that scorched earth); in any event, he did remain the last man standing, alone, on that field, for — in the meanwhile — we had relocated elsewhere. And yet, despite all their indifference or sincere animosity, no one will blot us out — neither my efforts and initiative to create a new poetic form, which I commenced in 1917-1919-1920, writing and publishing my verse in periodicals, and then collecting the same in the individual volumes *Green Eye* and *Electric Visions* (1920), *Night and Day* (1922), etc., nor my work as a visual artist aiming at the renewal of painterly form, along with the other members of the formist group — back when my exhibitions and those of my colleagues made our critics' blood to boil.

And now I offer a few of my narrative poems in opposition to the general intellectual cynicism which has taken hold of the postwar world, including Poland. Tossing palms on the tombs of our ideal, romantic poets, abusing elevated nomenclature in poetry, these are not steps in the direction of real poetry. It is cynicism, rather — one of the branches of cynicism that has reached into our literature as well. It is enough to take a close look at our literary relations, our sleight of hand and our bribery of elevated words and ideals; it is enough to come to know our social and artistic mendacity, to catch a whiff of that homegrown cynicism, that cynicism of phraseology.

And so, from romanticism to cynicism?

Through formism, I am striving towards a new poetry — to the liberation of the word from mould and cynicism.

(Warsaw, in August, 1927)

A Lajkonik in the Clouds

Poems

(1936)

The works of mine brought together in this collection come, in the main, from the years 1928 – 1935. Some of them have appeared in literary periodicals and journals — and one of the poems was even published, in its own good time, in the Cracovian *Switch*.

I take the opportunity here of confessing that, ever since that day when certain epigones of 'Young Poland,' conservatists and destroyers of 'poetic novelty,' sought to exterminate Polish futurism and formism (so fraught with significance for our most recent poetry, and non-poetry as well), I have decided to blaze my own trails in verse.

Our poetic 'avant-garde,' which would so like to distance itself from Polish futurism and so desires to relegate the latter's significance to silence, fortunately (in its works) is still under the influence of *Nife in the Stummik,* Bruno Jesieński's *Szela*, St. Młodożeniec's *Lines and Futuretimes* and my own *Green Eye* and *Robespierre*. All the better for them. — They have, at present, 'free range.' The range that we, the futurists, fought to obtain some fifteen years ago.

LAJKONIK

It was five o'clock in the afternoon
The hejnał was just bugled out
From St Mary's higher tower
The hejnał melody — a flood of trumpets
Which spread wide on all hands:
Glasses, and half-filled cups
Of coffee and tea
In the Sukiennice café,
Flowers in the flower-venders' pots
Set in rows over the cobblestones
Gillyflowers lilies and mums
Filled to the brim with the hejnał.
Above the Square above the Sukiennice
Angels
Two, female, in long white dresses
Soared, their wings humming like the summer breeze
And the harvester at rest beneath the trees
Harvests the thoughts of men
His heart — a poet.
And when the hejnał was cut off — then bells
Those friends of lonely people
Took voice from all the
Churches:
As from a radio station switched on
Bum bam — bum bam,
And all the thoughts of all the people there
Down on the Square, tangled
Thoughts flapped about the Square
Like birds — like white
Petals of flowers — like pigeons
White angels of birds.
On ulica Franciszkańska
Across from the rosy church
Of the Franciscans
A grey crowd gathers, Cracovian,
Pulsing with the blood of the fountain,
Hearts stroll about the cobblestones

Janglesounding
Blooms.
It's a bees' bazaar in the flowers
In the heavens' depths high above
The church, a flock of doves.
Above the bloody bastions of Waw-
-el a flock of daws.
And meanwhile:
From Dębniki to Powiśle
From the Półwsie Zwierzynieckie
One after another run
The Lajkonik's heralds
Each one decked out in strange attire
Neither Tatar — nor Turk
Of the XVth century.
Crested turban — azure shirt
And crimson gilligaskins.
Some of them even have wings
White or violet
They swoop down from the clouds
Along with butterflies
Like yellow-red butterflies.
These are the envoys of the Tatar khan
Of the lord of Zwierzyniec
Of the Lajkonik.
The crowd: cries and bustles.
This is a speckled serpent
Hissing
Sliding through the streets:
Students and hagglers, coachmen on fiacres
(With horses, muzzles in their feedbags)
Office stiffs solicitors and popes-of-fools
They push they crowd they cry.

HERALD I
People, hear me, everyone!
Gents and clerks
And those who work

And those who sell — tradespeople, come!
And draw about me in a ring
The news I bring is gay.
The Lajkonik is on his way!

CROWD OF LABOURERS
Hih, hih, hih.

HERALD II
Lajkoń the Great, our Lord
Has climbed aboard
His Pegaz, his steed.
Half-horse, half-toad,
He's an exotic breed,
Half-worm, half-bird.

CROWD OF MARKETWOMEN
Hee, hee, hee.

HERALD III
Our lord our horse — Laj
Is now close by
At Zwierzyniec there's an inn
Polish-Jewish-German
And at this moment, there he stands —
Mending the lining of his pants.

CROWD OF FIACRE COACHMEN
Hoo, hoo, hoo.

HERALD IV
Lord Lajkonik, of course
As if a hundred horse
Were bearing him quickly
Will soon arrive, thickly
Attended by his crew
Before the next hejnał's played through.

CROWD OF STUDENTS
Heh, heh, heh.

CROWD OF MARKETWOMEN
Louder and louder buzz the bees —
Rejoice, rejoice, gossips, grannies!

CLERKS
You hear the music? Here he comes,
As if from Zwierzyniec,
As if from Tyniec…

STUDENTS
You best can hear the basses grumble —
Like your stomach when it rumbles,
When you press it with your hands
And it thrums bars for a dance.

COACHMEN
Hear the horse a-neighing
Laughing, stepping, playing
Sounds just like my old grey nag
When her nose whiffs the feed bag.

CLERKS
With our binocles
We see where they're at:
Zwierzyniecka Street.
Soon the whole flock'll
Be here — like a cat
That smells meat.

And meanwhile:
The whole band
Is the Vistula foaming and gold.
First comes the Equerry
With shield of gold,
Followed by lackeys,

Magnificent drones.
Their large heads in turbans,
Red turn the cockspurs
To the very church doors
And prancing in the centre
Striking right and left, he canters
On his hobby-jennet Pegaz
(stuffed cowhide)
The Grand Goldbrick
of Zwierzyniec
King Lajkonik.
(At the sight, St Mary's two towers
bend in toward each other).
Despite the chaos of bells
Despite the doves
That dart in flocks
Like swarms of winged polliwogs
Beating the air
The two towers chat with one another:

LOWER TOWER
Have a look at how much fun
They're having, our Kraków burghers.

HIGHER TOWER
Have a look at how the skirts
Are spinning, twirling.

LOWER TOWER
O — and that dirty Tatar!
How proud he swells and skips around.

HIGHER TOWER
I've half a mind to go down
There, and with my golden crown
Smack that pagan stable groom
So, that he'll see stars and crescent moon!

LOWER TOWER
You'll see, you'll see
As, from the chilly cloister
Franciszek will go out,
That holy flower-monk
And give him such a clout
That'll teach the pagan punk
What it costs to roister!

(And the music plays, the music plays.
The crowd's a-buzz, and thick
Fall 'Vivat!'s and 'Long live!'s to the Lajkonik.)
Then at the Franciscan church
The mighty Lajkonik stands
A golden turban on his head,
A Turkish mace in hand,
With which he strikes out left and right.
The maidens giggle in delight
And the young men,
Quick witted, elegant,
Chatter a thin treble
And grab at skirts, bold devils.

AND THE LAJKONIK
Flutters the large crest of his turban
Spangling in golden rain
And jerking the golden bit
Makes his horse to halt and prance in place.
Tossing high his mace
Like a garland of diamonds
Heavenward
Making his oaken-coloured face to frown.
Then, fluttering his large whiskers
With stars his dark eyes shine,
His mace with grape tendrils is entwined.

LAJKONIK
All you assembled, everyone,
Gaze upon my awesome might.
I rule the tavern, dive and inn,
My gullet's deep, my maw is wide,
As Wisła's stream when it hits Gdańsk.
It's guzzled peasant vodka, and
Of noble wine it's deeply drank,
And now I and my faithful band
Are off to the Main Market Square
Before the bishop to bend the knee
And at Hawełka's place to feed
Our hungry steed,
And bow in reverence, lastly,
To the sister towers Mariacki.

BOTH TOWERS
(bowing)
Come here, come up close sweet khan,
You Polish-Mongol son of Ham,
And we will give you such a thrashing
That all your Zwierzyniec will be asking
'Who can he be, that pummelled man?'
Come here, approach, with all your band!

And then:
The narthex yawns
As the great bronze
Church doors spring
Wide, an eagle's wing
Each, or two great
Striped wings of a butterfly
Spread to sun and sky.
Between them a group of monks
With burning tallow tapers in their hands
With multicoloured lamps
And at their head
The poor saint in his patched robe,

Barefoot,
A thick cord around his waist
A grey asp
That writhes and clasps
Him about his chest
A zig-zaggy viper
That loops and capers
Shaking with zest
Its heart-shaped poll.
The saint's arms are all
Covered with wings:
Swallows, finches (gold and green),
Siskins, poor things
Fluttering, chirping, merry
Round the holy aviary.

SWALLOWS
Dear father Saint Francis
What are the chances that we
Might alight at the rim of your calvity?

SISKINS
And can we so perch
At your pockets, to search
There for seed
Upon which to feed?

SAINT FRANCIS
Flutter and seek, and eat your fill!
Just be careful not to spill
And spatter
White on my habit brown and dark!
The other monks — those turkey cocks
Think it a laughing matter:
'Look at Francis! How he walks
About, like a speckled crested lark!'

And so Saint Francis chats,
Il poveretto, with the birds
And meanwhile all the people
Have grown silent.
Some of them kneel and pray
Ardently.
In the silence
Flies are buzzing as they loop;
The leaves are heard to chatter.

SAINT FRANCIS
Hey there Mr Lajkonik
You sweet little beast
My dear
Come over here
And tell me your story
For God's pity.
Why do you race about the city
In such a hurry
Pushing folk, swinging that stick?!
You spook my birds away
And make such stir and fray
That even butterflies
Startled, rise
And from the gardens flee…
What's going on? Tell me

The Lajkonik draws close
And lowers the nose
Of his horse. He genuflects
In holy respect
Before the saint.
His turban he doffs,
He bows and bows;
Who was a boor, now's
A polite sort, sweet and tame;
All his monkeyshines and shame
He has cast off.

LAJKONIK
O my dear you cinnamon saint
You good old fellow
Don't forbid my bellow-
ing and romping there
Round the Sukiennice
Round the Square
Nothing beats a
Little spree on the odd day!
Let the people laugh a bit and play!
Look up there — just past the shutters
There fidgets a girl.
She wants to spin and twirl
Down here with the others
Like figures in a music box of gold.
Look, you don't scold
The birds that chase
The butterflies in their fatal race;
Nor do you marvel
At the pike when he sees a
Barbel
And spurts after him in the Wisła…

SAINT FRANCIS
Stop your lewdness
Unclean Lajkonik!
Because if you don't
I'll summon mother-Wisła
And have her overflow
And flood your Zwierzynieckie domains!
(calling)
Hey Wisła, mother Wisła!

Then down along Grodzka
From Wawel, from Kazimierz
A willowy maiden nears
In a blue silk dress.
In each hand she holds a

Pail of oak
From a water-yoke
Filled each to the brim,
And in each of them swim
Fish and crabs, all sorts of water folk.

WISŁA
O, just say the word, my father
And with my water
Over Zwierzyniec I'll spill
So, that he'll
Have a proper bathing,
That impious pagan!

CHORUS OF MARKETWOMEN
(lamentingly)
Hey Father, sweet and good,
Don't allow the Wisła to flood
Our fields!
How can a marketwoman deal
With that? And where
Will people buy their greens
When, on the Little Square
No marketwoman will be seen?

CHORUS OF FIACRE COACHMEN
O Saint Francis, Little Brother, Dear,
Should the Wisła flood our stables,
Where will we be able,
Poor coachmen!
To house our horses then?

CHORUS OF STUDENTS
If the Wisła floods Zwierzyniec,
So much for rambling in May to Tyniec...

SAINT FRANCIS

Calm down now, my people dear,
Nothing threatens, have no fear.
Mother Wisła, take your fish
And evenly, as always, swish
Between your banks.
And as for you, Sir Pranks,
Lajkonik,
Take your horse and take your stick
And make the people gay — but nice
And easy, so the devil
Won't arise
And spoil the revel.
And all you fish and birds and blooms,
Live happily, all
Who swim and zoom,
Who stand, who crawl.

The saint goes back into the church
Behind him all the monks process
With their tallow tapers.
The huge bronze church doors
Close behind them as they go,
Heavy, slow.
The music plays — the people dance
And sing.
See the Lajkonik prance
While, high above the city range
Squadrons of angels in aeroplanes
With wings of white,
Leaping and bucking around
The snares of clouds
Sailing towards the sun.
And as they danced and as they spun
Among them — see
The maiden angel of Poetry,
The friend of all
The poor and small.

HORSE IN THE CLOUDS

It started with flowers
Red roses and asters
Fields fragrant and woods
With birches and slenderest firs.
When my thoughts just like flowers
Or trees paling in spring
Winds and shivers erotic
And clouds, the violent embraces
Of the tangled arms of the sky.
And I lived then like a bird
Like the child of birds like a song
A dream buzzing over the fields
Of cobwebs of the strings of woodland fiddles
And then at the edge of the heavens
Above the mouth and skull of the mountains
The ring of forest and dream
Above the locks of birch plane and sycamore
Amidst a heaven of stables and gates
My pegasus galloped my foal
Over the ringing white cobbles of clouds
With fluttering mane from its hooves
Such thunder — a horse in the clouds
Of a spring thunderstorm — warlock and god.

JOURNEYS

From the gloomy mountain valleys
I entered life, from high darknesses,
From white clouds, shaggy cliffs
In the sky, from autumn mists
Above the golden leafage of the sycamore.

And then there were cities hot and squalid
Distant views of iron rails
Machines' white vapour trails and jewels — lamps
Electric in the long streets.

And then from distant seas there sailed close
Ships — white pods of dolphins
Amaranth mountains and ermine heavens
Volcanic smoky Tritons
The bastioned seas of the vagabond Ulysses.

And then I saw islands where grape
Vines — where wine spilled into jars
in Cana of Galilee
Where fish came ashore to impregnate
Virgins, the daughters of bronze islanders.

I saw floating bushes of coral
Inhabited by parliaments of gulls
White — broad cormorant waterplanes.
And at last I entered into a great city
Where among the rabble of people angels were deceived
By checkered cab crews on the avenues
This was a concours of fallen angels
Who were given prosthetic wings
And taught to fly in artificial clouds
Meanwhile the earth was unknown to them
Ever more unknown and alien
As if they were albatrosses broken by a storm
Perched on the mast of a foundering ship.

Autumn Spleen

High aloft through the heavens fly the storks.
In the church now toll the bells.
Yellow leaves from the lindens fly
In leaves of red are clothed the oaks
Above the waters thick mists swell
The yellow dawn glows in the sky
The sun's not laughing today, no
The stream's not bright with sparks, O no.
Through the pale stubble the lazy smoke spins
In the graveyard they're singing doleful hymns.

Against the grave's wall thuds the coffin
Corpse, all your days shall be forgotten
And the smell of the grave and the furrowed earth
The living breast and graveyard fir trees sigh
The soft song of the shepherds and drowsy reveries
And the black clouds that slowly sweep
And noisy nervous thoughts quickly fly
The rattle of leaves and faded memories.

(1906)

Warsaw at 5 in the Morning

The city dawn the clouds are flowers
Flowers thirsty for the dew like
Herds of bees in mountains full of blooms
The angels will fly off to Heaven soon
Pigeons of God flying off into the sky
Above the city down below the city moans
In sleep insects wake herds
People talk in their sleep pronounce
The bashful Name of God invoking
Angels the face of Lucifer fire
Burning in my veins as I walk the streets
On the corner I stand I rub my eyes
The mist a fountain trees in spring
People unknown to me walk the streets
On the corner I stand I rub my eyes
The autos and the lanterns drowse
The pale city drowsing blinks
With the gummy eyes of hope
Invoking on the street corner satan's name
In vain taking the name of that satrap
Usurper of criminals maidens sharpsters
In vain invoking that name dying
Perishing at the gate knife in the heart
And then the cops came marching down the left

Side of the sidewalk thick with blood
Where in the mud the little shoe prints
Of the pale girlish streetwalker
In the speeding auto at the wheel
A vodka bottle full and grey
The ghost is standing there laughing
All 12 centimetres of him tall
Meanwhile in the quiet Saxon Gardens
Where the last snow sugar melts at the wall's base
The dirty snow soot from the palace chimney
Beneath the snow pale green buds
The withered nipples of a young girl
Developing into chestnut leaves
A cat filthy with the soot of palaces
Hunter of the souls of birds and mice
Returns slowly a full montgolfier
Returns from nocturnal libations of love
Slips silently discreetly past the wall
That cat in fact is a Madrid sorcerer's
The famous painter Goya's from Quinta del Sordo
Here in Warsaw I know such a girl
Who's got a cat as white as a cloud above the Wisła
He's just fallen asleep on a bench on the Aleje
He was her livid lover
Thrice met by a police agent
The girl has a dress of pink silk
Like a spring cloud over the royal palace
At the dancing hall last night she drank some wine
Wine as tempting as the waters of the Wisła
The girl's breasts a tempting landscape of stillness
The spring wind flies along the boulevard and whistles
Hey automobile here to me quickly quickly
Calls the man in the shiny tuxedo and black
Fur coat like a tiger the fur in stripes
The car stopped on the long Aleje
Jerozolimskie that's the boulevard named
After the city where cross and palms
Awaited the youthful Christ

The cathedral organ rustles its wings
The child weeps in the cradle at his mother's side
Awoken from sleep as the dawn became
Warsaw the mother gets up to her child
In the hospital white cots stand in a row like the skiff
Of Charon with azure oars and bowl
Full of faded oboles
The scent of lysol cotton and camphor
Like clouds in the hall on the table
Wake people in rags
In the shelter in the den
Of the striped carcajou
A cloud entered an angel of blue
Through the ripped roof on a spring wind
A few flakes of melting snow flew in
These are the early butterflies of spring
Chasing the rose
Above the city an errant ray
Which the wind weaves among the clouds
Somewhere far far from the rising sun.

HAMLET IN THE CELLAR

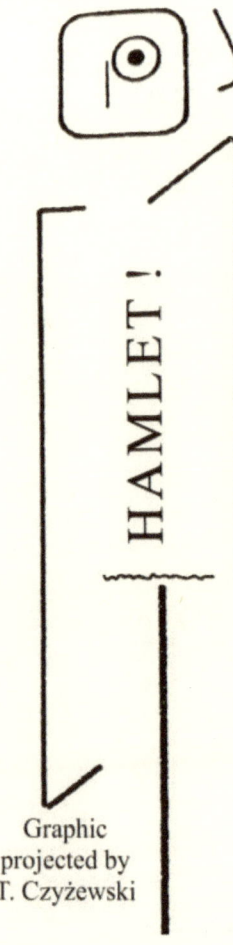

Graphic projected by T. Czyżewski

When once I took a walk down
into the dark cellar of my soul —

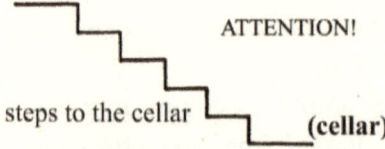

down the narrow stairs
I found a barrel there
     of old Polish malmsey
I didn't know that I'd be so poorly received

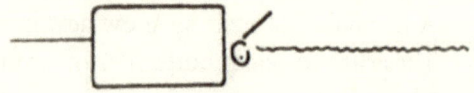

    by the king of the rats

For my soul is
Hamlet — half-deranged
she thumped against the humid walls
of the Dark cellar — Desert
Since I put no faith in the faith
     of my forefathers

The books of wisdom
with letters faded by the sun
    of stale wisdom

    a, b, c, d, e, f, g, h,

Hamlet!   **Hamlet!**   **Hamlet!**

let them just once let off
pairing you with Ophelia
I'll go down the stairs to my optical darkroom
to shred to pieces the tomes of my forefathers

PANAM

Panam Panam a beating heart
with its pulse that's a river within
and the blood that is sticky and hot
comes oozing down red silken streets
when I placed my hand on my heart
on the book living and warm
so as to read the living novel
whose title is Panam Panam
how often to spread one's wings
to fly into streets unknown
on friendly terms with the city
in love with its foul-smelling paths
the wretchedness ever so haughty
in the mud of the streets in the rain
to stand by the lamp on the corner
like a fake palm in a hotel
to be in botanical gardens
a rhododendron or a stone-pine
or in slippers second-rate
to play the role of the demon of night
how many times have I walked
your streets in the dusk O city
where the light-pools of shoreline lamps
sceptically tempt the shipwrecked
or passed on from Montparnasse
all the way to the Place de Clichy
to admire your smile you doll
in the mirrors of La Fayette
Panam, Panam in the dusk
the purest of harmonies, you
only in irony known
like all the beauties of the earth

AQUARIUM

from the nest of clouds which
hides behind the sun
        there flew on
fluttering wings
        embracing
the snowy fields of the sky
from open houses — green shutters
the glances of the familiar irises
of all the cardinal virtues
of inhabitants of seaside cities
        breadeaters
miniature, sinful little angels
        of the eyes
of the archangel gabriel
on powdered wings
of poodles shaved à la antoine
of people good for free
        and for a charge
for sport, *pro forma*
of fish swimming nose-blowing
        sharks eaters
of innocent mackerel and flounder
there sweep on ships great
        transatlantic
in love with puffs of the wind
and waves of pearly saliva
of a slippery lack of rhymes
and the poetry of rimbaud
and the poetry of apollinaire
sweep on galleys full of slaves
        with seals of violet
on their nervous shoulders
seals of equality, fraternity
        of the equality of slaves
in the depths of the aquarium
        submarine vessels
vessels full of the frowsty breath

       of mechanics
with prudent inventiveness
on the edge of the aquarium
grow little palms
miniature monkeys
swing there monkeys
with the tiny aquarial
        virtues
of miniature hypocrisy

A Verse on Painting

> Motto:
> All of painting, from the Greek frescoes in Pompeii all the way through Corot by way of Poussin, gives the impression of having arisen from the same palette.
> —Renoir (*Pensées*)

I saw the frescoes in Pompeii
In the Villa dei Misteri
The violet backgrounds harmonise
There with the black of the hair
The matte-rosy flash
Of the pearly female bodies
Painting is the harmony
Of sophisticated scales of colour
That live in the painter's eye
As a cloud lives in the sky,
As the reflection of a pale-rose lily
On the azure water of the pond,
As the flash of the wing of a butterfly
Against the dark blue
      Of a peaceful sky
Painting is a musical delight
Of the rarest tones, the simplest
From which the painter creates
      An image of the world
He couples on the surface of the canvas

    The rarest, simplest harmonies
        Just like
In its powerful
        Wealth
Unplumbed by man the harmony
        Of Nature.
And sounds and tones and form the painter
        Chooses
From the rich garden of flowers
And creates a new world
On his canvas
A world of inner harmony
That he senses and which
In him lives.

From the Concept of Nature — to Nature Itself

Contemporary art is presently entering upon a watershed era — especially painting (Poland, France, and Europe). (POETRY TOO).

    For some time now it has been said and written that art is not the copying of nature: Be that nature seen through the temperament, or the subjectivism of the artist applied to nature, or finally pure art. (*Creation pure?*)

    Nature is a constant mass (a body) — touched by the hands of a blind man. Touching things, the artist forms his own spatial world, upon which "CONCEPT" of his depends his very entry into the AREA of nature. That nature has the same effect on him as a lightning storm has on a pagan. Wishing to create for himself (HIS OWN) concept of a storm, he must turn to art.

    The recreation of a storm (the breaking of trees, wind, clouds, the sea) — or the ideal of abstract art? Let us imagine that the artist's relationship to nature (that surrounds him) does not in fact exist.

    So then, what is his relationship to pure forms and their reciprocal influences upon one another? [geometric forms — forms half-geometrical (mixed) flat and spatial — the arabesque]. Through abstract form — the artist approaches nature — since he must return — in order to discover his own spatial world — in order to be in the midst of that lightning storm — and not just view it, observe it, from the outside.

So, identification with nature? — NO!

To create one's own world from nature — not an abstract world, but ONE'S OWN.

A sculpture, a building, a painting, a poem — this is not an identification with nature, it is NOT THE ABSTRACTION OF SIGHT — it is nature, unconditionally itself. Materially and spatially individual. HARMONICALLY DEPENDENT upon the centre of the lightning storm (nature) in which the human being (the artist) finds himself.

This relationship provides the work of art — with the harmonic laws of the environment of the natural storm — the laws of nature herself — with relations of grandeur and pettiness, with relations between the types of material (the relation of weight and attraction — analogy).

Pure creativity as it is now understood — does not exist. ABSTRACTION: is therefore dependent upon the environment of the storm (man is nature) and as such is the slave of nature — forms — even abstract relations cannot exist outside of nature. Man proceeds slowly and executes movements — which defend him from disappearance in nature (physical nature).

The machine is not nature — it is an instrument for the obtainment of the ideal of nature itself — which is art.

Disinterestedness plays no role — in art — nothing plays any role in art which is not me MYSELF — who creates an IMAGE or a poem, WHICH IS NATURE ITSELF, not identically but in the centre of the lightning storm.

ZARAGOZA ZARAGOZA

the town grows silent
to speak with a bell
with a pigeon's wing
with hyacinth blooms
Zaragoza Zaragoza
with a rosy wave
a stripe of incense
the Madonna's face
black whortleberry
Zaragoza Zaragoza
Goya his portrait
from battles distant

from distant coffins
death in a frock coat
Zaragoza Zaragoza
in the arena
of our Lady's town
the blooms come alive
the stripes of coral
Zaragoza Zaragoza
corrida lily
palms of hyacinth
searching for pearls
crimson raspberries
Zaragoza Zaragoza
they found velveteen
the bleeding roses
butterfly-eyelash
the Madonna's eyes
Zaragoza Zaragoza

A Barcarolle from Seville

early morning I caught sight
of three songs of three azure nymphs
on the calm sea three purple clouds
three ships with purple sails and shrouds

on the copper drumhead of the sun
I thumped my ringing symphony
in vain the sea all full of fish
tossed up its transparent billows

the calm upon the sea then cast
a veil upon a young bride's brow
and sharks between the hips were wound
into a wreath with mimosas

mimosas flowers of yellow
the fragrant airports of the bees

while bells from all the city spires
rang out furious obsequies

a sprig of thought a chrysalis
coloured like butterfly cutworms
crawls on its path like an auto
a limousine on wheels of silk

the vesper bell's already chimed
the fishermen alight their lamps
upon the sea a yearning sails
a jeered-at sentiment of romance

a black-haired doña in mantilla
and swarms of butterflies that fill a
cage some red some grey some rose
up in the mountains dancing roads

upon the cobbles dance the roses
and hair blooms thick with mignonettes
romanticism creeps from the bastion
the moon's on the gates of Sevilla

I pound on the gate with a hammer
surely my memory serves me well a
chest here holds the manuscript
of a romance that I've secreted

my thoughts that gnaw upon the flowers
upon the wall the flowers wither
the crickets of the field prance
in the costumes of marionettes

these are my thoughts that gaily dance
the strings of a guitar are hissing
not vainly sea and yet in vain
the talisman of my passion

it's easy to arouse the bells
the flowers will shortly bloom again
the roses and the black carnations
in mourning for their princess passed —

(Seville, in October 1929)

Birds

In the cathedral of Toledo, where
Christ hangs, battered and bloodied, from his hair
His crown of thorns fell. It rolled round and round
until His Mother stooped, and picked it from the ground.

She picked it up, that Mother sore distressed,
cradling the bloody thorns against her breast.
The thorns bit through her flesh, and they bit deep,
So that the blood through her blue cloak did seep.

Some doves were startled at the bloody sight
of thorns sunk deep into that bosom white —
at which, they flew to Mary's breast in droves
to pluck therefrom those thorny stilettos.

Then, from a far-off land flew in swallows
to help to ease the Pure Mother's sorrows;
and from green fields sped in lark after lark
to soothe the pain that tore the Virgin's heart.

O darling birds — your labours are in vain!
Nothing can ease the Doleful Mother's pain;
that pain is nothing to the misery
those nails give her, hammered into the Tree…

More painful than flashing stiletto blades
are her Son's eyes, where the gleam of life fades;

more than her heart, by thorn and sword now riven,
she suffers for the wounds her Son was given...

In the cathedral of Toledo, where
Christ dies, a flock of birds wheel through the air.
Hush now, hush now, don't flutter your wings so —
Take each a thorn into the world now, go.

Roses of Andalusia

In Andalusia the roses bloom
the roses bloom amidst the flames
torn were they in the night by storms
inside the stones were breaking hearts
upon the cliffs eagles, like dreams,
plucked at their pennons with their beaks
to sign a pact with the kingdom
of the proud Aragonese queen
the Moors had settled in their courts
stroking the fountains' swelling breasts
while roses chatting with the sun
awoke the sailing ships from sleep
the pirates pillaged the shoreline
the rose — blood from a thorny wound
climbs slowly up the Cross's pole
where Christ opens his parched lips
thirsting to sip the rosy dew.

Guitar ribbons

Ribbons of a guitar and love
where the sun dressed in leotards
bathes in the sea early morning
and love a winged butterfly
seeks out delight among the blooms
the heart takes fire with the dawn
and is extinguished when dusk falls

when the sun sails about the sea
when the smoky mountains are snuffed
and the thuribles of the flowers
and the loud buzzing guitar strings
the humming ribbons of guitars
in and throughout the alleys white
the toreador-moon steps in
to rattle his guitar like leaves
opening the window shutters
he gives the blooms venom to drink
the ribbons transform into snakes
he wakes the owls — butterflies.

Grenada

Among the groves buzz harp strings
Generalife
the music of the mountain streams
lush flowerbeds
of the Caliph
like Eastern infernos the walls are red
cypresses
of the Albaicín
The Churches are arrows of celadon
in the taut bow in a giaour's hands
the holy words of the Koran
carved upon the fortress walls
words of crime and doom
Mendoza's cross and the crescent moon
streams
tiny insects
babble in the leaves
and silence is the mother of delight
amidst the quiet
rattles the string of amber
on the bosom of Alisha, bright
star of the harem
of Alhambra

CORRIDA
(A BALLAD)

For Marcial Lalanda

Lalanda's sabre flashes
in the sun a viper mad
and the bull a cloud of black
with streamers of bloody rain

¡Hombres! Lalanda calls out
like Roland to his servants
give me another sabre
a ray of Mithras divine

the banderilleros run
great butterflies of yellow
they swarm the bull with ribbons
rainbows flaming bluebottles

the silence seeps in the blood
Lalanda pierces the heart
blood flows out the bull's nostrils
cascade of Alpujarra

his comrades run up to him
Manuel Aguilar 'Rere'
Francisco Chaves 'Chavito'
to shake the hand wet with gore
Lalanda's viperish hand

light the gold tallow candles
he says to these his brothers
before the Señorita
for her prayers of thanksgiving

the chapel candles glowing
the large eyes of Madonna

stare like two jet-black embers
at the blood-soaked Lalanda

the blood poured on the sand a
blood-token of my glory
blood with which I would wash clean
the painful wounds of Thy Son

the blood unites with the earth
the doves fly up to heaven
from the arena-altar
of the great god Mithras.

Flower-girl in Seville

Seville, Plaza de San Fernando
a tramway of green arrives
the flower-girl is bearing bouquets
of violets and hyacinths

These are for you señores
these for you señoritas
in every violet there's hid
a drop of love, like honey

love is born in flowers
love is culled from flowers
be bees my señoritas
be butterflies señores.

Eulalia Waits upon her Daughters to Give Birth
(a ballad)

Three daughters has Eulalia
three virgins ripe and robust
like three apple trees
Tra ra ra

One's in love with a grape vine
Another for the almond pines
And the third is in love with the sea
      with the sea.

Nuptials beneath the pomegranate dome
of heaven, with grape vine and almond tree
and with the frothy stallion of the sea.

Three daughters got with child

      Eulalia
(the fisher's wife) rejoicing claps her hands
The one gives birth to grapes as heavy as
      heaven's pomegranate.

The other bears fruit as fragrant as the eyes
      of Naiads, Naiads —

And the third:
Was to bear a Triton a little Triton
      but she's dead.

      (O woe is me).
In the frothy sea — abed drowned she.

      Mercy.

NATIVITY PLAY

(Prologue)

Over mountain over vale
over forest over dale,
four stars have been set alight
two moons now are shining bright,
through the valleys rivers play

like vipers sliding down the brae
clouds rush up the summits steep
as at pasture flocks of sheep,
through the trees birds spread their cheer,
in the woods beasts shuffle near,
in the valleys to the bothies
people near are drawing;
at the foothills by the dark trees
flocks of sheep are baaing;
in the valleys music plays,
rebecs and jew's harps make a din,
people slide up in their sleighs
to the crowded huts and inns.
Something's happening down there,
Something festive, something rare.

— — — — — — — — — —

TRAMP
What's that humming, what's that jangle?
Like a wedding — who's got tangled?

JASICA
THAT MUSIC THERE IS FOR BETHLEHEM.
THE SHEPHERDS RAISE A JOYFUL MAYHEM;
THE SHEPHERD GIRLS ARE SO TRICKED OUT, WOULD
PONIES BEAR THE WEIGHT? I DOUBT IT.
   (THE ROUT WITH BASH
   AND BOOM AND CRASH
   SENDS THROUGH THE BEECH
   SONG, THUMPING FEET.)

THE ROUT
Bu – bu – bu – bu
Berries red and berries blue
Hu – hu – hu
Through the beechwood, hey! Right through!

TRAMP

That you're not consumed with sadness
here among these mountains high.
That you all laugh, loud with gladness
and your joy sounds through the sky!
That your soul's not weak and whining,
that your flesh is strong, not pining,
that you're all content, like doves,
or like the holy saints above!
That you look so hale and hearty,
ruddy, sprightly, strong and swarthy!

JASICA

Here we've music, dance and game,
here we're off to Bethlehem —
Such is our nature — understood?
Sons of mountains and the wood,
We soar like eagles, wantonly;
Like to the fox and wolf, we're free.
From joy to sadness — half a mile
Or more! We've our own tongue and style.

GROOMSMAN

O my people, O my people
how life passes by!
O my mountains, O my mountains
poking through the sky!
O my birds, my royal birds
who skim the heavens high!

BRIDESMAID

O my fish, my sprightly fish
who through the waters flee!
O my waters, O my waters
rush on to the sea!
Gone, be gone, sadness, away!
No mourning here shall be.

Fly past the mountain far away,
to the drab city flee!

THE ROUT
Slowly now, hush, leave off that stomping,
Music, lighter now, leave off your romping.
Softer saw your whining fiddles,
tone the flutes down just a little…
Now, the bass! Again be pounding!
Set the happy racket sounding
to bring the news to Bethlehem
that joy will never abandon them!
Let Joseph and the Virgin hear
the while they rock their little Dear.
Let little Jesus laugh, to know
the mountain people love him so!

— — — — — — — — — —

BETHLEHEM
(Manger)
And there in the manger, the stable, the hay,
kneels the Virgin, and Joseph, a little away
to the side. The Child Jesus — a sweet little doll! —
sleeps there near the stool in His crib in a stall
while Maria sings Hush Baby, hush, lullaby,
and the puffs of white smoke from St Joseph's pipe fly.
The angels are there; down from Heaven they glide,
beating their wings, like peacock-tails pied.
The wood pigeons have come, swooping down from the crest
And the black cocks who bow before the Maiden Blest.
Near the crèche in the stable the ox shifts and stirs
and the ass, the poor fellow, he champs and murmurs.
Both the ox and the ass kneel them down by they crèche
to keep the Christ Child warm with their soft purring breath.

THE ROUT (stops in front of the manger)

STAROST
We've crossed the Dunajec that tumbled and swirled
we've travelled the roads to the end of the world
to stand at the manger here on the threshold
to bow before God, just a few hours old;
we've come with fair words and with music to play —
if you greet us with gladness, why, here we shall stay.
And here on the porch are the gifts that we've brought;
now we'll play and we'll dance here before the Lord God.

THE ROUT (plays)
O my basses my fat basses
thunder, split, like the cliff faces!
And you, fiddle, little fiddle,
as a wren trills in a willow,
get your strings to chirp and hum.
Hey, my flutes, and lutes!
My kobzas, come!
Strum and thrum and twirl
and let the bagpipes skirl!

GROOMSMAN (before the music)
Around the porch I'll spin and dance.
I won't be like some oaf that stands
Still and lets his girl sit on her hands!

BRIDESMAID (before the music)
How eager now he is to dance!
I'm his — don't you go making plans!
He's jealous. See those fists? His hands
Ain't just for shooing flies like fans!

BACA (before the music)
When the winds die down, the meads
grow silent, then I'll drive my breeds
and goats up Cicha there to feed,
but now żeńtyca do I carry
to refresh the Virgin Mary.

BANDIT (before the music)
I brawled in Mikuláš and Spiš
and there the justice of the peace
would write me up and send
me to the clink…
But where's his ink?
And where's his pen?
He's got none, for my sturdy fellows
swiped them from underneath his nose!

BEAR (before the music)
Don't think it odd to see me here
a fat black bear
dancing and singing
sweating and swinging —
I've breakfasted on half a deer!
But let the hunters not attempt
from Hamry to chase me,
'cos on Smreczyńska once again
they'll have to face me!

HUNTER (before the music)
If not for Jesus in his crèche
I'd dance you to the death, the death,
but there He lies in manger bright —
we'll have no quarrelling tonight.

ORGANIST (to the Rout)
O brothers, beasts, O wretched ones
who've got less coins than you have thumbs,
be nice now! Let's have no more jars.
Be in agreement, like the stars
above in Heaven — come, shake hands,
be humble, as the Lord commands.

Meanwhile THE ROUT DANCES
(MUSIC PLAYS)

Add your voices to the song
as well as you may, before the dawn.
Come, everybody, dance around
the manger, feet thudding the ground —
Look how the baby Jesus smiled!
Saint Joseph and the Virgin mild,
that, poor and wretched though you be
still do you dance for them with glee.

— — — — — — — — — — —

TRAMP
As the earth has need of sunlight
as the stars spread over her at night
with love toward that same sun burning
so man for light is ever yearning.

JASICA
The earth before the sun bows low
Above the earth, the hosts of stars aglow
Gaze on the sun with love's delight
Just so the men of earth rush to the light.

— — — — — — — — — — —

SHEPHERDS (running up)
Hey people, people, something's going on!
Above the crèche, a star — big as the sun!

SHEPHERDS (running up)
Some army's coming close — wagons and vans;
Some sort of toffs draw near over the sands!
    (The Rout looks on
    without a sound
    up in the sky
    the sun spins round)

THREE KINGS
Draw up the vans,
the four-in-hands,
with servants and bell
and blackamoors as well,
gold-sack and torc
of splendid work —
set it all down now
before Jesus, and bow.

CASPAR
We come from distant lands
from farthest oceans' strands
at the great star's behest
through river, through forest.

MELCHIOR
We're led here by the star
past river past wood, far
we've come to kneel before
the King who's lain in hovel poor.

BALTHAZAR
Gold, myrrh, and frankincense
we offer as presents
with many a good word
to Jesus, the Good Lord.

THE STAR
(Rises above the manger, above the ridge-pole, above the roof. Everyone kneels; the star makes a bow before the crèche and glows.)

I wander through the sky
collecting light, for I
would shine for Jesus bright
as the sun this Christmas night.

--- --- --- --- --- --- ---

AT THE MANGER
Then they bow low, the magi-kings
and prostrate, too, their underlings.
The pennons flutter, camels kneel,
the music plays — the shepherds reel.

--- --- --- --- --- --- ---

EPILOGUE
In that blest hour, way back when,
in that manger in Bethlehem,
the kings, the drones, the animals,
the poor folk were rejoicing all.
With music playing, songbirds singing,
sun and moon and stars down flinging
gold into the humble stall.
With joy the world went faster wheeling,
with joy the little Babe was squealing.

(Paris — Warsaw 1926)

Mysterium

The oaks with autumn once golden,
By the winds of winter now torn,
Standing lonely in the field,
Are lashed by the bullwhips of snow.
But the sun like a golden ducat
Tears through the dark clouds and displays
A sky blue as the depths of a lake
Suddenly in the mountains revealed.
And the moon shines bright toward evening
And the stars off the rushing pane
Of the mountain freshet reflect,
A stream rapid that sputters and snorts
Like a frenzied stallion plunging

Against the cliffs' granite footing.
The villages slowly grow still
The evening star beckons on
To the manger, the fragrant hay
Through the soughing winds gravid with all
That the mountain leas once bore.
The moaning oaks now grow quiet
The snow-covered pines now grow still,
Above, the torn clouds are speechless,
The swift-flowing streams do not roar.
Amidst all the silence, like strings
Of a harp sublime music was heard.
It's a choir of beautiful singers —
Winged, with wings like the sun.
There's a manger, and straw from the flowers
Which bloomed on the meadows in summer.
Above it the Mother is bent
To rock her sweet Child asleep
And the angelic-butterflies
Shine amidst the deep snow like rainbows.
All the animals kneel at the crèche
While the shepherds arrive with their music —
Harmonica here, kobza there,
The carpenter Joseph they see,
The Virgin and Child they greet.
Who opened wide the doors — so wide
To let the impish wind inside
To twirl and swirl in sprightly glee
Knocking against the high roof-tree?!
Who was it set that star to glow
And who're those people, who now go
Across the porch in robe and gown
Before the Child to kneel them down?

— — — — — — — — — —

Hey birds and angels, shepherds, magis,
Clouds and stars in the deep skies,

Snows in the ruddy twilight,
This night, here in this mountain crèche,
Before the King of wretchedness,
Hand taking hand in a firm grip
They join as one in fellowship.

Canticle
(mysterium)

Peace from a heaven full of lights
flows down to earth, into the vales
covered in snowdrifts and in frost.
And there in the deep mountain valleys
below the jagged ridge's rim
forests of thick fir trees grow dim.
But there's a lean-two bathed in light
and full of fragrant hay and straw,
and in that shed the Mother sits
pressing her Child to her breast…
      A crowd of birds is gathered there —
a flock of winged angels bright.
The mountain streams are sounding, roaring loud;
the woods are humming near the mountain tops.
The sky is caught in spiders' webs of clouds,
and birdsong rings throughout each brake and copse.
The fieldfare whistles in the junipers
and eagles screech about the rocky spurs
aloft; below, a crowd of poor folk goes
crèche-ward in frayed trousers and battered clothes.
From Spiš they come, and from Ujhel…
and wandering buskers jangle near as well
(the sort that through the Slovak country prowls
from wedding to wedding) — flute chirps, bass growls.
Behind them come some farm-hands, all worn out,
jacks-of-all-trades, and soldiers, such a rout
of them, millers and sawyers, and no lack
of handy journeyman and lumberjack;
some groomsmen from a wedding (saucy fellas)

and gorgeous bridesmaids — Różas and Anielas.
Some too, who fight the strong to help the weak:
the comrades of the bandit Janosik,
From Łomnica, Orava and Mikuláš,
who, from their early years left home, and rushed
into the woods; Sabała too did come
(of all the fiddlers, he second to none);
from distant lands the three magi-kings came:
the first among them Caspar was, by name,
Melchior, Balthazar, the other two,
with gold, myrrh, frankincense and pearls too.
When all before the manger had arrived,
pauper and monarch knelt down, side by side.
They saw the Child asleep amidst the hay,
the animals all kneeling down to pray;
they heard the cooing of the mourning doves
and saw the stars bend down low from above.
And love, which in the hearts of all is found,
like a rich pearl sunk many fathoms down,
brought to the surface, broadly did expand,
encompassing each planet, sea, and land.

A Naive Nativity Play

for Stanisław Piasecki

The earth and all the stars of heaven
circle like a flock of sheep
and the sun, at his morning shift
smiles to all the clouds and stars.
In the valleys, the evening calm
wanders round on owlish wings,
and in the mountain meadow high
a poor manger stands in the snow;
and to this manger people run
through valley, over mountain stream,
across the aged summits grey

in frost and ice quite locked away.
And in the manger, Mother, Child,
both rest their heads upon the straw —
dried stalks of the most fragrant flowers
brought from the green oaken woodlands.

. . . .

BACA
Now everyone, come, at this hour
gather, and to the shelter come:
farmers and shepherds, journeymen
from far and near, come everyone.
Let each one take what each one might
as gifts, whatever his cellar yields
and with a foot both swift and light
take it up to the mountain field.

SHEPHERD
What road will lead us to that place,
and why are you in such a hurry?
What's happened there? Why must we race
there, for God's sake? Why must we scurry?

BACA
And did none of you hear the news,
my people, O my people dear?
That in the manger there up high
the King of the poor is born at last!
And what rumour had prophesied
has in all truth now come to pass!

MATEUSZ
They say that all the valley birds there flit
to sing and warble to the Child a bit...

WOJCIECH
They say among the wolves there's been some talk
of gathering for Him a nice fat flock...

AGNIESZKA
The Jews in Krościenko market said
— if rightly I understand it —
that the Orava bandits
have bought some golden pillows for His head.

SHEPHERD KUBA
And I — four cuckoos to the Child will bring!
The angels on high will laugh to hear them sing.

BACA
Enough of all this jawing and vain fretting —
Look at Świnica, see? the sun is setting,
and you're all standing here to gape and drool
just like a flock of sheep around a pool.
Meet me up at the manger, everyone —
and bring your sheep-flocks with you when you come,
before Virgin and Child to humbly bow…
and don't no one overlook Joseph, now.

. . . .

And so they all ran up to the high wood
where, in a clearing, deep in the snow stood
the manger, where the Infant Jesus lay,
warm in his crèche, amidst sweet-smelling hay.
And all around, in rafter and roof-tree
the winged carollers, perched, they did see:
bunting and finch, turtledove and siskin,
bullfinch and mourning dove, and wood pigeon,
and high above, with bright wings like rainbows
sat the angelic musicians, in rows…

There also came kings from afar,
three: Caspar, Melchior, Balthazar.
They all bowed low, in that poor room,
spreading their gifts; the angels tuned
their harps and lutes; the birds began
to squawk and sing as best they can,

and everyone on that high field
joined in. They played, they sang, they reeled,
poor little Child Jesus for to praise.

. . . .

and from the high heavens, down the stars gazed
in pure delight, shedding their sparkling rays.

A Nativity

The fish of the Dunajec, salmon, trout
Through stoney-silver currents dash about,
The beechwood rustles leaves yellow and sere,
In the thick dusk the mountains disappear
Toward Slovakia — Havran and Muran
Are frosty grey — about their base expand
Forests of spruce with trapeze-skirts of white.
Hey baca — hey there baca, it's been years
Since you built that lean-to up here!…

Baca

The years have quickly flown, like a cuckoo through the wood.
It seems we've just been born, and soon we're gone for good.
I built that manger, a splendid hut on the high plain —
Today a Gentleman stays there along with his train,
His wife Maria and their little Baby Boy.
He's just been born today, that little bundle of joy!
His little arms, his little legs, just like a doll's, so gay —
Some serving-folk from Rój were just asking the way
There to my hut, to visit the Baby today.

Dunajec Fishermen

Hey baca tell us, tell us quickly now, brother,
Where can we do homage to the Child and His Mother?
We've got some silver barbels here, and some spotted trout,
Some graylings, chub and sanders that we've just fished out
Of the swift stream — how do we get to the manger there?

To set before the crèche this gift of modest fare?
The punnets of fish that we're bringing to Our Lady —

BANDITS
Hey there baca, hey you old Robin Hood,
Show us the way too, for we would
Like to bring before the Lord with haste
This little deer — the booty of our chase,
And there behind us, with some other loot
Our mates: who've caught a wolf by the foot
And from the Homolac wood, a whole stag
That without aid of dog or flint they bagged.

BACA
Ha ha ha ha ha what a sight!
That wolf's beside himself in fright!
That sure will make the Baby Jesus laugh
To see that grey barbarian that you've gaffed!

MUSICIANS
And tell us too, baca, show us the way
To the crèche in the manger where Maria stays
With the Child and the joiner Saint Joseph; to them
We'd do homage with flute, bass, and with violin.
We'll play them a sztajer, a csárdás and so
Onto waltzes, for which you need a nimble toe.
And then we'll play the march that old Rakoczy
Had them play when he'd been tucked in bed nice and cosy —

BACA
And then the bandit's march, like when Janosik
Set out from Hruby, that time he went to seek
The feast at the wedding of the Luptaks,
Pummelling on his way there five Ludźmirzaks,
And neither the pandurs knew, nor did the cops,
And he burned down four taverns before he stopped.

SHEPHERDS
Hey baca, you great old man, say if you please
Where's the road leading up to the high mountain leas
Where in his straw-filled crèche lies the Baby
And there beside Him, His Mother, our Dear Lady,
And the carpenter in his old trousers and torn jacket —
We'd like to go see them. Each one has a packet
Of cheese, a mendel of eggs, and a brick
Of butter. And what's more, Black Kuba's picked
A nice ram that he leads by the horns and the fleeces
To give to our Lord, the newborn Baby Jesus.

BACA
To that poor manger, the path goes
Across the stream, through the windthrows,
Then through the meadows, then turn right, mind you,
And there at the shack at the wood's edge you'll find you.
So be on your way with your gifts and your horns
To the manger where lies the Christ Child new-born,
And I'll follow you up after a little space
But first I must change my frock and wash my face.
See — the evening comes on and the stars are all out;
The skies sparkle with them, and the moon swiftly mounts
As the sun sets beyond the woods off to the west.
See? The moon with her sickle now pricks that cloud's crest.
So be off, little folk, to greet the newborn Child,
Up the road here, and let that there star be your guide
What you see blinking there when the fluffy clouds part —
It's the same one that leads the Three Kings from afar.
Caspar, Melchior, Balthazar — that's what they're called.
Who they are, where they come from, you'll find out, and all
That they've got to report, when you're all gathered there.

The evening folds herself in the grey air,
The mountains grow still and the winds
Die down, as that most holy night begins.
The hearts of all the humble pound with joy
To greet the advent of the Blessed Boy.

As Alpine streams swell down the mountainside,
The yearning heart with love, at last, is satisfied.

Shack in the Mountains

On the mountain meadows lilies bloom
the violets of snow and clouds
the forests rattle their casque of green leaves
and fiddles sound — the strings of the winds
an old woman's memories of a shack
hidden in waves of snow in the depths
of distant mountain ribbons mountain ranges
those buzzing hives of bees are firs
they sound anew, pale music of the lyre
along the ribbons of the paths through vale
to ridge the spurs of granite a creeping throng
hastes rushes rushes flocks of sheep like ants
the dogs bark, their voices carried on the wind
about the mountain meadows like the blows
of hammers blows of steel on stone
the cries of shepherd the songs of birds
the cantillating firs organs in church
the golden jangle of keys of copper
bells in snowy temples
and in a little crouching manger
among the mountains amidst the dark azure
stains of distant woods and ochre hamlets
in the bothy where a trough of gouged spruce
holds fragrant ringlets of herbs
a flock of sheep baas in the racemes
and cows hoot like owls at nightfall,
in the crèche a Baby mills His arms
His Mother kneels leans in over Him
lost in the bright wells of His lash-ringed eyes
the Baby peeps the forest birds peep too
the most lovely music to her ears
it flies up to the clouds the silent crags
Joseph the carpenter stands at the porch

in an old ramskin coat a staff in hand
lost in the heavenly blue of ridge and lea
the music of the clouds upon the wind
and past these clouds are shining swarms of stars
like pins, diamonds, pearls or bees in swarms
or fireflies on St John's Day the sparks
of distant shepherds' bonfires roasting pits
the icy ridges of the Tatras, clouds
seeking to chase about with the moon
from village and meadow from clearing from hamlets
of grey cottages crowded with smoke and folk
they come in droves with music ringing
like beetles buzzing bass and flute
the snow-thick clearings bloom like orchards
lost in their gazing at the Child
His mother His manger and the star
a glowing nail in the blue sky
pierces the thatch the roof the beams
to make the grey stable to glow
Child and Mother and shepherd crowd
transforming the snow into flowers a cloud
into spring's veil a warm fresh breeze
before the crèche the star then leads
up king and shepherd from high above
Bethlehem's harbinger of love.

An Unintelligentsiaed Saint
(fragment)

WISE MAN
(stands at the seashore
the sea billows the Sun
    sparkles)

life is built up like a song
like a birch cane
of many thin stiff fibres
thrust in the ground it blooms

with green eucalyptus leaves
the saint who is unable
to bear life in cloth of gold
without crotchet hook without stiletto
with which to core the human breast
like the earth made red by the sea
boulders bald giant shoulders
of plough of ships furrowing the sea
he shuffles along a snaky path among the cliffs
snuffling the air like a wolf
striking the world with his eyes like an eagle he
stands at the seashore
greets the billows
greets the gulls touches immensity
looks around
and breaks the sea in half
searches its depths where the coral
grows looks to the shore
where roses bloom and dahlias.

THE SAINT
(in rags walks along the path and talks
to himself)
I saw the loaves pass by this way
toward the city to the market for people
O some bread — give me some bread
it is so hard when hunger wakes
I wanted to save that hunger for myself
as one secretes one's sordid thoughts
when the soul no — but the body in need
when life arrives at a crossroad

WISE MAN
(to saint)
like mountains are the loaves of bread
golden brown at the summit
only he shall get some bread
who has employment for his need

THE SAINT
(tossing his habit from himself, is naked)
this hand sought violence
this leg kicked a bosom
this finger pointed mockery
this nose sniffed flattery
this eye hissed with contempt
this mouth lied love
this bosom pressed wanton
these thighs shivered like bells
at the grand carnival of lust
these haunches were like slicks
at the great bordello of life
this body frothed with foam
like a swine a muddy puddle
(he falls to the ground)
beat me, beat me
I want to know who I am...
(the crowd surrounds the saint and gapes)

ONE IN THE CROWD
Come on crawl out of this has-been man
crawl out from that sea of dirty foam
the back that once lay
on an eiderdown on a melodious bed
the sea of the body that flowed in billows
in the bay of the great pig
(he kicks him in the bosom, on his back)
the Saint gets up and gets dressed
and walks along the seashore deep in thought
and the Crowd follows after him.

On the Delogicalising of Poetry

The first, main task of contemporary poetry and prose is the elimination of the word from its enslavement to the logics of phrase and syntax. This has nothing to do with the symbolism of the word, i.e. with the bestowal upon the word of some planted, or artificial, or even tectonically accepted meaning. The word in poetry or in prose possesses a realistic meaning, which is autonomous in relation to other words set next to it, or even, eventually linked to it by the logical interpretation of thought.

The liberation of the word from the purely rational, 'thought'-based fog and casings has occurred only over the space of the last few years, when contemporary (most recent) poetry strove to break through the wall of 'logicality', fatasmagoria and arbitrary naturalistic interpretation.

For example, when we pronounce the word 'horse,' we see in our thoughts (according to the logical materialisation of the word) — the logical auricular-verbal bestial interpretation. According to the old poetical conception, 'horse' is also a synonym for running, war, a noble and sublime elevation — and this idea reaches as far as symbolism and the symbolic conception of the word 'horse'. Should we add an attribute (an adjective) to this word, for example 'winged' = winged horse, we see how logically, idea-logically, and even symbolically, the word horse has been transformed, somewhat — even strengthened imagistically, conventionally, in a poetic sense.

Let us imagine that a poet of the *ancien régime* (the old model), in composing his elevated term adds: **in the clouds** to **winged horse**. Here we have idea-logically, logically, and imaginatively, an entire picture painted in the old technique, with all of the 'chiaroscuro' and retouches of a Raphael or a Salvator Rosa or in fact the sublime narrative poems of Byron. It was Romanticism that endowed the logical expression of syntax with its most elevated and most idealistic significance.

Verlaine and Mallarmé thrust the logical idealism of romantic syntax into the symbolistic thickets of poetic expression via the syntactical images of formulaic logicality.

To the romantic idea there yet mixes in the use and application of **onomatopoeia** — borrowed in any case from ancient Greet poetry — from the conversations and exhortations of the heroes of Homer. With this one difference, to wit: Greek poetry employs onomatopoeia with greater simplicity, often quite 'autonomously' — according to the general exigencies of that hexametre. The Romantics, on the other hand, made of onomatopoeia a music, corresponding to the 'mood' of the verse.

The poetry of the French Parnassistes, and that of their modern epigones, exhibits a particular mastery of purely logical verse expression (even the poet Paul Valéry was jammed into its strictures). The first poets who attempted to free themselves, whether from the iron 'logicality' of the Parnassistes or the logical, symbolical plants of Mallarmé were: Marinetti, the inventor of 'Futurism,' and the French Cubist poet Apollinaire.

The one and the other began to use the word, I reckon, automatically, unthinkingly even, only for its innate value as such, what I call its 'autonomous' value. Let us suppose, for example, that horse, for them, is no longer either the absolute interpretation **of the logical imagination**, nor an onomatopoetic sound evoking the image of a horse (*Pferd — cheval* — the labial snuffling of a horse) — but a word autonomously and conceptually constant, fixed.

Proceeding from this assumption, we may presume that each and every word possesses its own **autonomous** value (be it a spoken or a written word) demarcating its values logical, conceptual, or finally auricular-onomatopoetic. The word, in and of itself, cleansed of pseudo-values (which after all do not describe its sonoric-linguistic meaning) — automatically possesses value only in itself, and becomes the foundation of a new poetry, a new prose. Let us take, for example, the primitive poetry of the Negro and the peoples of Oceania. We shall find there (Blaise Cendrars: *Antologie négre*) a like motif and a like solution. Sounds, as for example (we assume) ai, aüo, ao, and so forth, employed meaninglessly (as far as logical words are concerned) can function suggestively as poetry: as evidence we offer = war chants, and Negro songs at funerals and weddings. The word as sound, or in general as an autonomous whole, has a suggestive value and only as such may it be used in poetry. If we take, for example, a certain number of words and by means of so called **anarchisation** link them together, providing them with autonomous, suggestive meaning, giving them in their gathering (the phrase) a lesser, or greater, logical or imaginative significance, we bring them closer to **the essential meaning of the word, as poetry**.

In the introduction to my *Robespierre* (1927) I wrote: 'I endow each word that appears in my poetry with individual significance and autonomy; at the same time via the anarchisation (not anarchy) of words, separating them into groups of analogous words, from which I elicit analogous phrases, etc. For this reason, words and phrases, despite a frequently superficial alogicality, as a whole (through the contrast of bonding materials) result in a cohesive entity, which lives like an organism in the natural world.' the complete break with what had been up till now the 'logicality' of poetry, under whatever term it was known:

Romanticism or Symbolism, leads to the creation of **suggestive poetry**, the poetry of **true realism**.

The word, as a sound, or as a suggestion, as the essential voice of nature: the song of birds, the voices of animals, the songs of aboriginal peoples — is the foundation of the poetic autonomy of the word, which leads to completely new, broad possibilities in prose and poetry.

(1929 Collioure, Pyrenées orientales)

Scattered Poems

Spring 1917

To the memory of the poet Apollinaire

Earth I invoked time and again
today the sun is a great wound
from which the knives were withdrawn long ago
Caesar Borgia that clown in scarlet
and the hunchbacked shadow of Richard III on the wall
gaze at the crumb of moon sticking out
        of the shoulder-slung satchel
swallows glide over the dome of the sky
spring flowers blossom in the fields
clouds form up into warring armies
I see Alexander the Great
        from the Pompeian mosaic
armies with banners emerge
        from the trenches of Verdun
while far off among the clouds of spring
the dark artillery helmet of Wilhelm Kostrowicki takes shape
an armoured train rumbles through the sky
a thunderclap of spring shivers the earth
to its very bowels its rotten bowels
to the very beating heart of man
the storm makes a great tree to bend
that leafless stands in the field alone
the fecund green of the virginia creepers
climbs up the blackened trunk

Realists

I am no dreamer not me —
says Wencel the bookkeeper
hunting flies on the table
he's sweating in that jacket.

Dreaming is a plague a sickness
it does away with trust —
the president tells him
picking at a hole in the drawer.

Clouds wander about the skies
like accounts in a ledger
the prez stares at the ceiling
Mr Wencel sticks his nose up his sleeve.

Today is the thirtieth
Mr Wencel tells himself,
tomorrow is the first —
the prez babbles in his soul,

and thus soberly they converse
two humble realists
meanwhile the flies escape
to the warm tiles of the stove.

A Little Town

Like a brooding hen with her chicks
the little town rests, amidst wood and field.
Its streets are blue, green and white.
A messy cat spurts into the butcher's shambles.
The butcher — fat tyrant of lamb and cow
rolls up his sleeves, and lights a long pipe.
The butcher's pipe gives birth to white clouds
and the clouds in the sky are
the sun's flock at pasture.
And now once more — a horse or two

pull an empty cart along the street.
This is the mayor's vehicle.
The mayor is a man
who plays bridge every Saturday
in the little town's casino.
Two red and white flags flutter above the casino.
Tomorrow on Sunday afternoon:
a ball for the orphans of the unemployed.
There will be vanilla and chocolate ice creams
(let's hope the sun tempers its scorching beams)
there will be dancing and a soloist, it seems.
Already today
the cashier
of the food cooperative
has gone to bed. He
wants to be ready
for tomorrow
but a gramophone
from the floor below
won't let him alone:
'Love, don't weep,
I have time, I'll wait.'
But he can't sleep.
Great.

Lang Syne

(BALLAD)

For Kazimierz Tetmajer

The little moon in hazy sunlight disappears,
From Ludźmierz manor, Mr Tetmajer draws near.

To him the mountains from their rocky summits bow;
The firs, and the slender sycamores too bend low.

Hey hey! There's nothing like the freedom of the hills
Dunajec sings, as over the cliffs he spills.

Mr Tetmajer stands on the rocky scree
In fetching cap and cape — he's quite the sight to see.

And then, gazing up the sharp and sloping peak
Tetmajer mused, and thus, gloomily, did speak.

Down from the jagged Kościeliska heights
In shining armour come a-rushing, knights.

Above Świnica proud, above Krywań
The eagles soar on wide-spread, whooshing van.

The knights rush through the windthrows of felled stone,
And in the thick mountain mists, from sight are gone.

In the smoke-filled shack, amongst the flocks of sheep,
The garrulous baca our company did keep.

Long has it been lads, hey! a long time since
We last went after the black grouse with our flints!

After the black cock, the chamois swift of foot —
And we'd come back with sommat', that we would!

And then a-Sunday at the Krzyżów inn —
The Halkas and the bandits would dance and spin!

And once on his way from Krosno, our poor friend
There on the rocky scree met his sad end.

For Death prowls on the rugged mountain crests
And yet the bandits? They could not care less.

These Tatras' glory spreads now through the world
Since first Tetmeyer his epyllions skirled.

He sang and on the summits cast his eye
Where freedom soars, like an eagle, through the sky.

Freedom, liberty, and the sun of gold:
Apollo's three-in-hand, snorting, prancing bold,

Just like that stallion that past the Tatras darts
Spraying Podhale with his thunderous hoofbeats' sparks.

Autumn Night in Batignolles

At the bus station
at Rue Legendre in Paris
I was waiting for a ride headed
to the Boulevard du Montparnasse.
The Paris autumn went its misty
way among the stars,
shining with the light of electric lamps
shining with the stars of the Milky Way.
The grey wind swept along the street
dirty sheets of paper
old wrinkled gazettes
that turned somersaults
like circus clowns
playing with the autumn wind.
Above the basilica of Sacré-Coeur
on Montmartre
arose the moon.
The same moon as once
20 years ago
lit up a winter night
above the Carpathian woods.
Back then there was a sleigh
ice and snow crackled beneath
the runners and an icy
wind blew down from the mountains.
I scented the aroma of burning

kindling and branches seeped in resin,
the white clouds
slid through the winter sky,
quietly slipping
into the sleepy voice
of bells.
The sound of the sleigh-runners
slipped like a stiletto
through the veil of silence.
The white bus stopped:
Gare Saint-Lazare, Madeleine,
Concorde,
Bellechausse.
The trees along the boulevards
shimmered with decrepit gold
the houses bared the burnt teeth of their windows
streets of nocturnal mist
hung above the city.
Right now in the Carpathians
in my home village
the moon rises above the woods and hamlets,
that bus of a moon.

Ballad of the Organgrinder

The organgrinder
with the wooden leg plays,
the green parrot
is in the wire cage,
he turns the crank
in the Wisła-side mists
at the threshold of the bridge
where the river waves shine.

I once had a wife
(so his melody goes)
and my wife had a son
a wee little one

like a little snowball
rolling through grass and dew
he had birds in his hair
and butterflies too.

And then came the wind
from the Wisła so cold
and then came the sadness
of winter days.
The sill-potted blooms
blossomed with the frost
and the flowers met their doom
in their cold clay pots.

Dear passer-by
would you hazard a try
your future to see,
your destiny?
For five grosze mere
the green bird here
with his crooked beak
will pluck what you seek.

His green feathers
are like groves in the spring.
With his crooked beak
he plumbs the future
the day of death:
but you will live long.
You'll become as rich
as Rothschild himself.

And the parrot squawked,
the clouds will float
above the Wisła in a boat
and your time passes
like the autumn wind
and the organ grinder with the wooden leg

turns his crank
sings and plays.

I once had a wife
and my wife had a son
a wee little one
like a little snowball
rolling over the grass
and then came the wind
the winter wind…
alas.

In the windows flowers
of ice and glass
and on the floor a wooden casket rests
near the Wisła
banks near death…
So the organgrinder
with the wooden leg
sings and plays…

TEXTUAL NOTES

The Death of the Faun

—Original title: *Śmierć Fauna*.
—Village Alderman: *Wójt*.
—'Despite his age he still can rage.' The original old saying in Polish: *Stary, ale jary* (roughly: 'old, but still potent.' We translate the same saying later, in the Faun's song, as 'Although I'm old, I'm still a bold one.'
—Faunalia. Ancient Roman holidays dedicated to the god Faunus (vide infra). They were held twice a year, in mid-February and early December.
—Faunus. According to Schmidt, Faunus was one of the earliest indigenous gods of Rome, sun of King Picus and grandson of Saturn. A forest god — clothed in goat skin, but not necessarily with horns and cloven hooves, which were only attributed to him when he was conflated with the Greek god Pan. In Roman mythology, he inhabited forests, fields and streams, was a protector of herds and agriculture. His oracles were transmitted through the movement of branches.
—*Faune, Nympharum fugientum amator...* from Horace, *Odes* III:18. 'Faunus, lover of fleeing nymphs / through my borders and through my sunny fields / may you enter benignantly, and depart propitious / to the little offspring of my flocks... / if at the end of the year a tender kid falls victim / and abundant cups of wine / the companions of Venus, are not lacking / and the ancient altar smokes with much fragrance. [...] The wolf wanders among the fearless lambs...'
—*Štajer*. A folk dance originating in the Slovenian regions of the Austrian empire, or Styria, hence the word, a corruption of the German *Steierer*.
—*Faker*. Hired Hand Kuba calls the Faun a *Ciarach* — a term that denotes someone putting on airs; a peasant trying to pass himself

off as a townsman by dressing the part. The other peasants, like Kuba, reckon that there's something inauthentic about the Faun; that he's not what he seems to be, and is dressing himself up in order to disguise his true intents. Thus, when the pummelling begins, they call him a 'changeling' (*odmieniec*).

—*A whole nation.* 'Nation' (*naród*) is sometimes used colloquially to signify a crowd of people. One might say 'Look at all the people!' in Polish via *Ale narody!* That's the primary meaning of the word here. Whether or not Czyżewski is making a comment on the *Polish* nation is unclear. The fact that Kuba responds 'We're a noble nation!' to the Faun who calls them a 'rabble,' is a reference to the Polish myth of Piast, the first king of Poland, being a commoner, and may lend some credence to the supposition.

The Green Eye. Formistic Poems. Electric Visions

—Original title: *Zielone oko. Poezje formistyczne. Elektryczne wizje.*
—Zofia Ordyńska (Zofia Pindelska, 1882–1972). Actress associated with both the Juliusz Słowacki Municipal Theatre and the Bagatela Theatre, both in Kraków. Kryszak and Waśkiewicz tell us that she took part in the poetic evenings of the futurists, where she recited the verse of Czyżewski, among others.
—Jan Piotr Hryńkowski (1897–1971). Painter, one of the founders of the Polish expressionist and futurist groups. He also worked in theatres in Silesia (Katowice, Sosnowiec) as a stage decorator. Some of his poetry was published in futurist publications.
—Leon Chwistek (1884–1944). Painter, theoretician of art, polymath. He lectured on mathematics at the Jagiellonian University in Kraków and the Jan Kazimierz University in Lwów. One of the most important theoreticians of the formist movement in Poland, his *Wielość rzeczywistości w sztuce* [Plurality of Realities in Art] is especially noteworthy.
—Ferdynand Hoesick (1867–1941). Publisher, journalist, literary and musical scholar.
—Tadeusz Boy-Żeleński (1874–1841). Physician, writer. One of the most notable Polish literary characters of the early twentieth

century, Boy is noted for his quick-witted satirical poems, many of which were written for the famous Cracovian cabaret 'Zielony Balonik' [The Little Green Balloon], collected later into the volume *Słówka* [Little Words]. He wrote many important articles dealing with Kraków, especially the Young Poland years, and was a prolific translator of French literature.

The Snake, Orpheus and Eurydice. A classical vision.

—Original title: *Wąż, Orfeusz i Eurydyka. Wizja antyczna.*
—*Dynamopsycho*. A term coined by Czyżewski. It seems to refer to the 'dynamic psychic' energy that motivates the poet, crucial 'moments' of which are caught visually in the stylised illustrations to the right of the text.

Donkey and Sun in Metamorphosis. A formo-satirico-bouffonade

—Original title: *Osioł i słońce w metamorfozie. Formo-satyro-buffonada.*
—Marian Szyjkowski (1883–1952). Professor of Czech Literature at the Jagiellonian University in Kraków. Later, he held the chair of Polish Literature at Charles University in Prague. While in Kraków, he directed a dramatic school (these are the 'literature courses' to which Czyżewski makes reference in his introduction to the play), and founded the Bagatela Theatre, which still exists today.
—Actors of the Bagatela. These include Wanda Trojanowska (1883–1949) — fined after World War II for appearing in the boycotted official theatre during the occupation, and Jadwiga Kowalikówna (??), who, according to the *Encyclopaedia Teatru Polskiego* [Encyclopaedia of the Polish Theatre] at the time worked as an extra at the Słowacki Municipal Theatre. Henryk Heniowski (??) was a member of the company at the Bagatela in the 1920s; the Broński in question is probably Zbigniew (??) who is credited with appearances in two Bagatela productions in the early 1920s. I have been unable to identify M. Łukasiewicz and M. Leszko.

—Stanisław Młodozieniec (1895-1959). Poet. Along with Czyżewski and Bruno Jasieński, one of the founders of the futurist group in Kraków. Following World War II, he lived in London before retuning to Poland a few months before his death.
—Zygmunt Waliszewski (1897-1936) was a Polish painter involved in Kraków Futurism, but in his work mostly influenced by post-Impressionism.
—Maria Jarema (1908-1958). Also known familiarly as 'Jaremianka,' she was an important abstract painter. As a collaborator with Tadeusz Kantor and his Cricot 2 Theatre, she is an important link between the early Kraków avant-garde of Czyżewski, and the later, postwar avant-garde of Kantor.
—The donkey rattles off a literary pedigree of authors from the time of the ancient Greeks who made use of the animal fable. As for the Poles, Ignacy Krasicki (1735-1801), is Poland's greatest author of the Enlightenment (see his *The Mouseiad and Other Mock Epics*, recently published by Glagoslav), Władysław Prokesch (1863-1923) was a literary critic, as were Stanisław Pieńkowski (1875-1944) and Emil Haecker (1875-1934), both of whom were none to friendly to the Futurists. Jan Pietrzycki (1880-1944) and Władysław Kosicki (1879-1936) were poets. Karol Irzykowski (1873-1944) was a writer and a critic, whose 1903 novel *Pałuba* (*The Harridan*) is sometimes compared to the writings of Joyce.
—Szmaja. Perhaps a reference to the oculist and multi-talented musician and artist Stefan Szmaj (1893-1970), associated at the time with the Expressionist journal *Zdrój* [The Spring] based in Poznań.
—Paweł Staśko (1892-1943). A popular naturalistic novelist of the early years of the twentieth century. According to Kryszak and Waśkiewicz, Staśko had a wide audience among the 'kitchen help' — hence the reference to 'cookbooks.'
—Orgelbrand's lexicon. Samuel Orgelbrand published an encyclopaedia in the late nineteenth century.
—Maciej Szukiewicz (1870-1943). Poet and theatrical critic.
—Kazimierz Bartoszewicz (1852-1930). Publicist, publisher and literary scholar.

—Ubi genus ubi rura / Sic asinum vocat natura. 'One's country makes one's person; thus the donkey is called by his nature.' Basically 'you can take the boy out of the gutter, but you can't take the gutter out of the boy.' The second line is in Polish in the original: *Jak widać osła ciągnie go natura* [as is obvious, the ass is drawn by his nature].
—Bruno Jasieński (1901–1938), Anatol Stern (1899–1968), Aleksander Wat (1900–1967), futurist poets, the latter two Varsavian, friends of Czyżewski. Besides his poetry, Stern is the author of an important study of the Polish roots of Guillaume Apollinaire, Czyżewski's poetic master. Toward the end of his life, Wat was interviewed by Czesław Miłosz. The result was a thick book entitled *Mój wiek* [My Century], a fascinating document of Polish history and literature during the twentieth century.
—Pilec. A town in north-east Poland, far from both Kraków and Warsaw.

A Burglar of the Better Sort

—Original title: *Wyłamywacz z lepszego towarzystwa.*
—Café Bullier. A brasserie in the Montparnasse section of Paris, named after François Bullier (1796–1869), a Parisian lamplighter, who founded the Bar Bullier.

Night — Day. The Mechanical Instinct Electric.

—Original title: *Noc — dzień. Mechaniczny instynkt elektryczny.*
—Mażana, Dziewanna. Ancient pre-Christian figures from Slavic mythology. Mażanna (or more properly Marzanna) was a death goddess, Dziewanna an agricultural deity. The ritual of drowning Marzanna, by tossing a festively dressed effigy of the goddess into a river — which is supposed to ensure a good harvest — is still practised today in certain parts of Poland. Of course, it is more of a holiday than anything — something akin to the burning of the Guy on Bonfire Night in the UK.
—*l'avion de mon corps adoré* [the aeroplane of my golden body].

—*mon cor criant dans le bois* [my horn crying out in the woods].
—Ola Föns. Probably a comic misrendering of Olaf Fønss (1882–1949), a Danish actor and director, who starred in Danish and German films of the silent era. Czyżewski throws the reader even further off the scent by transforming the masculine name Olaf into the feminine Ola — a Polish diminutive for Aleksandra.
—Mia May (Maria Pfleger, 1884–1980). Beautiful female lead in German silent films from the same era.
—Eustachy Kajetan Sapieha (1881–1963). Polish statesman, Ambassador to Great Britain following the reestablishment of the state after World War I, later Minister of Foreign Affairs.
—Sukiennice. The mediaeval cloth hall; one of the most famous buildings on the Main Market Square (Rynek Główny) in Kraków.
—Ulica Szewska, Ulica Długa, Ulica Wolska. Streets in Kraków.
—Wyraj. In Slavic mythology, a paradisiacal region to which the birds fly off in the winter.
—(the rat goes slowly the Doppelgänger). The line is ungrammatical in Polish, too: *szczur idzie z wolna sobowtór*. With punctuation — a comma after *idzie*, the sense might be 'the rat goes along, slowly the Doppelgänger [goes too].'
—God is no. Again: in Polish 'There is no God' would be *Boga nie ma*. Instead, here we have *Bóg nie ma* ('God is no.') On the other hand, *Bóg nie ma* can be a sentence fragment: 'God has no...' lacking a direct object. We prefer the ungrammatical ambiguity here.
—Lajkonik. A figure dressed in Turkish garb, who, astride a hobby-horse, prances about Kraków in a traditional celebration on the octave of Corpus Christi.
—Adam Mickiewicz (1798–1855). Romantic poet, the national bard of Poland. the 'Ode to Youth' [*Oda do młodości*] is one of the most famous poems of his early years. His *Forefathers' Eve* and his *Sonnets* have been published in English by Glagoslav.
—Wilhelm von Tegetthoff (1827–1871). Austrian admiral, widely respected for his strategical talents.
—Prince Józef Poniatowski (1763–1813). Polish military leader, nephew of Stanisław II August Poniatowski, the last king of Poland. He served in the Austrian Army, the Polish Army, and the Grand Armée of Napoléon.

—Andrzej Pronaszko (1888–1961). Polish painter and scenographer, associated during the early twenties with the Formists.
—Lalo. Although Czyżewski often includes onomatopoetic sounds in his verse, in this case, we have an untranslatable pun. 'Lalo,' which rhymes with 'hallo,' can be the vocative form of the word 'Lala,' which means 'doll' in Polish (although most people prefer the diminutive form 'lalka').
—Furrore. *Sic*, 'furror' in the original Polish.

Pastorals

—Original title: *Pastorałki*.
—As a generic term, 'pastorałki' is difficult to precisely render into English. Generally speaking, 'Pastorałka' is a Christmas play, or dialogue, with a long tradition in Polish, the earliest reaching back to the sixteenth century at least. However, certain Christmas carols are also referred to as *pastorałki*, particularly those set in the mouths or milieu of shepherds (hence the name). Czyżewski makes little distinction between the musical *pastorałka* and the dramatic *pastorałka*. Thus, depending on the sort of verse presented, we render it variously as Carol or Nativity Play, though at times we just leave it as Pastoral — which is the term used most often by English commentators. It may have a bucolic ring, but as Jan Okoń points out in his collection of *Old Polish Dramatic Pastorals* (XXXIV, *ff*), as classical as the form may be, the southern Polish setting of the pastorals, with their familiar, homey tang (something that Czyżewski, a native of the Tatras, capitalises on), gives the bucolic genre a very indigenous, Polish feel.
—*Kolęda*. A Christmas carol per se. This is the original title of the first poem in this collection.
—Bachleda, Opiela. Common surnames from the mountainous regions in the south of Poland.
—Baca. A senior shepherd.
—Kierpce are slippers common to the mountainous areas near the Slovak border.
—Kobza. A lute-like instrument.

—Kulig. A sleigh party; somewhat like a hayride, with song, and bonfires, and drink.
—Kaciary-maciary. Nonsense words, but with the ring of a spell.

Robespierre. Rhapsody. Cinema. From Romanticism to Cynicism

—Original title: *Robespierre. Rapsod. Cinema. Od romantyzmu do cynizmu.*
—Scriptures. The word used in Polish is *Pisma*, which can range in meaning from journals and magazines to the Bible.
—Catherine Théot (1716-1794). Supposed French visionary, with delusions of grandeur, who mixed a peculiar interpretation of Christian imagery with an adulation for the French revolution — in particular, with Robespierre, in whom she saw a redemptive figure. Made use of in a plot to bring down Robespierre.
—Juliusz Słowacki (1809-1849). Polish romantic poet and dramatist. His play *Kordian* touches upon many of the conspiratorial and martial themes mentioned in this section of the rhapsody. (This play, and several others, is available from Glagoslav). In 1927, about the time when Czyżewski was composing this poem, Słowacki's remains were transferred from Paris to a crypt in Wawel Cathedral, Kraków, where they lie next to those of Mickiewicz.
—Siklawa. A waterfall in the Tatra mountains.
—Young Poland. *Młoda Polska.* The dominant poetic and artistic movement in early twentieth-century Poland, preceding the First World War. Considered by some a modernist movement, it has more in common, perhaps, with nineteenth-century Romanticism. It is marked by an interest in folklore and peasant motifs, and its linguistic tenor, which favours dialect and neologism, is considered by many to be cloying. It produced one truly great poet, the dramatist Stanisław Wyspiański (1869-1907). Some of Wyspiański's plays are available in English from Glagoslav.
—The journal Czyżewski mentions was *Formiści*.
—Tadeusz Peiper (1891-1969). Polish avant-garde poet.

—*The Switch. Zwrotnica.*
—'City, Mass, Machine.' The title in Polish builds in a pleasantly alliterative manner: *Miasto, Masa, Maszyna.*
—*Squares... Kwadraty* was published in 1925, and *Słowo o Jakubie Szeli* in 1926.
—*Nife in the Stummik. Nuż w bżuhu,* a large brochure issued on 13 November 1921 containing work by Czyżewski, Jasieński, Młodożeniec and Anatol Stern. The title itself is a 'futuristic' and provocative attempt at a phonetic simplification of Polish orthography (the proper spelling would be *Nóż w brzuchu.*)
—The youngest poets. Czyżewski uses the adjectives *młody* (young) and *najmłodszy* (youngest) in preference to *nowy, najnowszy* (new, newest).
—Jan Lorentowicz (1868-1940). Polish literary and dramatic critic.

A Lajkonik in the Clouds. Poems.

—Original title: *Lajkonik w chmurach. Poezje.*
—Most recent poetry. As earlier, Czyżewski uses *najmłodsza* (youngest) here.
—*Lines and futuretimes. Kreski i futureski (1921).*
—Lajkonik. Lajkonik refers to the main character of a particularly Cracovian event, which takes place each June, on the octave of Corpus Christi. It is then that a person dressed in a fantastical 'Turkish' or oriental style, with a long fake beard, a tall pointed cap, and a gaudy hobby-horse fixed around his waist, dances and prances from the Zwierzyniec section of the city to the Main Market Square. Attended by song, he skips through the crowds, striking people left and right with his staff of office (the *buława*). (Whomever he strikes is glad to be tapped: it brings good luck). According to legend, the Lajkonik procession, which has its basis in the frequent conflicts between Catholic Poland and the Muslim East (Turkey, the Tatars, etc.) dates from the thirteenth century. Konik means 'pony.' The etymology of laj is a bit more obscure, though some see it as the imperative of the verb *lać*, 'to beat, to strike.'

—*Hejnał*. A famous trumpet call in F, played to all four directions from the higher tower of St Mary's Basilica on the Main Market Square of Kraków, each and every hour of the day. It is one of the most recognisable symbols of Kraków, and is transmitted live on Polish radio each day at noon. The trumpeter is a member of the Kraków Fire Brigade, as the higher tower of St Mary's was traditionally used as a fire-watch station for the mediaeval city. The melody is abruptly cut off — legend has it, that the *hejnał* was first played as a warning by a watchman, who saw approaching Mongol hordes stealing up to attack the city in the thirteenth century; a Mongol bowman silenced the trumpeter with an arrow through the throat.

—Ulica Franciszkańska. Franciscan Street, a street in the mediaeval centre of Kraków, down which the Lajkonik traditionally makes his way to the Main Market Square.

—Wawel. The ancient royal castle in Kraków, on a hill overlooking the Vistula (Wisła), which has been inhabited since prehistoric times. Besides the caste, the Cathedral Church of SS Stanisław and Wacław is located here.

—Dębniki, Powiśle, Półwsie Zwierzynieckie. All locations in Kraków associated with the progress of the Lajkonik. The Lajkonik begins his journey into the centre of the city from Zwierzyniec, where those people who traditionally comprise his suite are located. Dębniki is a section of Kraków across the river from Zwierzyniec; Powiśle is a street leading from Wawel hill to Ulica Zwierzyniecka.

—Tyniec. Site of an eleventh century Benedictine monastery, down the Wisła from Wawel Hill, past Zwierzyniec. A popular destination for pilgrimages and Sunday walks.

—Hawełka's. A café restaurant on the Main Market Square in Kraków, founded in 1876 by Antoni Hawełka.

—Grodzka. Ulica Grodzka, or 'Castle Street;' part of the Royal Road which runs from the Barbican, through St Florian's Gate and down St Florian's St (Ulica Floriańska), through the Main Market Square and up to Wawel Hill, Grodzka being its last section.

—Kazimierz. The historic Jewish quarter of Kraków, past Wawel, leading to the Wisła River.

—Little Square. The Mały Rynek, a smaller square stretching behind the Main Market Square (Rynek Główny) and bordered by Ulica Sienna, Ulica Świętego Krzyża and Ulica Mikołajska.
—The Aleje. Aleje Jerozolimskie — a main Warsaw thoroughfare.
—Breadeaters. *Zjadacze chleba*. A phrase first used in 'Testament mój' [My Testament] by Juliusz Słowacki, in which the poet suggests that his 'fatal power' will continue to work on the generations of his countrymen 'until it transforms you breadeaters into angels.'
—Pure art. While Czyżewski may be referring to the nineteenth century theories of Gautier, i.e. 'art for art's sake,' the Polish ear catches an allusion to the theories of 'pure form in theatre' set forth by Stanisław Ignacy Witkiewicz ('Witkacy,'1885–1939). Witkacy was briefly associated with Czyżewski and the formists. However, his theatrical works had a strong influence on Tadeusz Kantor, who likewise drew from the prewar Cricot Theatre and Czyżewski for his stage creations.
—The centre of the lightning storm. What we translate, approximately, as 'centre' in Polish is *Ośrodek* — i.e. centre, hub, environment.
—Guitar ribbons. Literally, *wstążki gitary* ('ribbons of a guitar').
—Marcial Lalanda (1903–1990), Spanish bullfighter. Other practitioners of the cruel sport are mentioned in stanza five.
—Nativity Play. *Pastorałka*.
—Jasica. A male role. Dimnutive of Jaś (which is itself a diminutive of Jan).
—The Rout. *Wesele*. The word usually designates a wedding feast, which in traditional Polish milieux can last three days. For this reason, two of the characters are designated *drużba* and the *druhna*, which can mean 'groomsman' and 'bridesmaid.' Here there is no wedding per se, unless it be the 'marriage' of Divinity to humanity in the Incarnation of Christ; the word *wesele* derives from the same root as *wesołość* ('gaiety,' 'jollity'), and so it should be understood here. The Rout will have a speaking part; whether this be intended as a composite role for a group of revellers, or a personification of the jollity, is unclear.
— From joy to sadness — half a mile / Or more! We've our own tongue and style. *Od radości do smutku u nas pół mili, / bośmy słowami sami się uczcili.*

—Starost. *Starosta*. A village official.
—Before the music. *Przed muzyką*. This may indicate that the speaker (or singer) stands in front of the band to deliver his or her part, or that the verse is delivered a capella, after which the music strikes up, leading from one verse to another, where it pauses again. Or, it may indicate both.
—Żentyca. A sort of kefir made from sheep's milk, known in both Southern Poland and Slovakia.
—Spiš, Ujhel, Orava, Mikulaš. Towns and regions in Slovakia. The Tatra mountains form the border between Poland and Slovakia — but as in all such regions, national boundaries are rather arbitrary things, and the mountaineer cultures of both slopes have closer bonds to one another than the Polish mountaineers have with Warsaw, the Slovaks with Bratislava or Prague, or Vienna.
—Róża, Aniela. Female names, common at the time of writing.
—Juraj Janosik (1688–1713). A highwayman, who has entered into both Czecho-Slovak and Polish legend as a type of Robin Hood.
—Sabała (Jan Krzeptowski, *also* Sabalik, 1809–1894). Celebrated fiddler from the mountainous regions of southern Poland.
—Stanisław Piasecki. Unless the addressee of Czyżewski's poem is a personal friend unknown to history, there are two Stanisław Piaseckis who may have received this dedication. The first, Fr Stanisław Piasecki (1885–1962) was a Catholic priest who studied for the priesthood in Kraków, served a parish in Tarnów, and then emigrated to serve the large diaspora of Poles in Brazil. The younger Stanisław Piasecki (1900–1941) was a literary and theatrical critic of nationalist leanings, friend of the poets Tadeusz Gajcy and K.I. Gałczyński, one of the founding editors of the review *Prosto z mostu* [Straight from the Bridge, i.e. 'straight from the horse's mouth,' or 'Plain Speaking']. He was murdered by the Gestapo in 1941. Czyżewski placed certain of his poems in *Prosto z mostu*, which leads us to believe that it is the younger Piasecki to whom this particular poem was dedicated.
—Świnica, Svinica. Like Havran, Muran and Krywań, a mountain in the Tatras on the border of Poland and Slovakia.

—A Gentleman. In Polish: *Pan,* which can also mean 'Lord.' One is tempted to see a reference to Jesus here, but the poet is obviously speaking about Joseph, hence 'gentleman.'
—Old Robin Hood. *Baca harnaśny* — the adjective is formed from the noun *Harnas,* a term in the dialect of the Tatra mountains denoting the chief of a band of brigands.
—Csárdás. Hungarian folk dance, widely known throughout Slovakia.
—Luptaks, Ludźmierzaks. Ľupták is a Slovak name; Ludźmierzak is a reference to someone from the Polish town of Ludźmierz. In the original, Janosik doesn't only burn down four taverns and beat up five Ludźmierzaks, he also kills three *harendarze* [or *arendarze,* tenant-farmers].
—Pandurs. Irregular armed forces, which at times policed Slovak regions in the Austro-Hungarian Empire.
— A mendel of eggs. An old traditional unit of measure. As a dozen = 12, a mendel = 15.
—*An Unintelligentsiaed Saint.* Title: *Odinteligentiony święty.*
—*On the Delogicalising of Poetry.* Title: *O odlogicznieniu poezji.*
—Idea-logically. *Pojęciowo.*

Scattered Poems

—Spring, 1917 [Wiosna 1917r.]. Published in *Prosto z mostu,* 1936.
—Wilhelm Kostrowicki. The birth name of the French poet Guillaume Apollinaire (1880–1918; full name: Wilhelm Apolinary Kostrowicki — hence his Frenchified nom de plume). His mother was a Pole of a noble family; his father is unknown. He volunteered for service in the French Foreign Legion at the outbreak of World War I, and was wounded in the head by shrapnel from an exploding grenade in 1916. He died two years later from Spanish Influenza.
—Realists [Realiści]. Published in *Prosto z mostu,* 1936.
—A Little Town [Małe miasteczko]. Published in *Prosto z mostu,* 1936.
—Lang Syne [Drzewiej]. Published in *Okolice poetów* [Poetic Regions], 1937. The title 'Drzewiej' is an outdated Polish term for 'Dawniej' [long ago]. It is the sort of regionalism or archaism that appealed to the poets of the Young Poland period, such as Tetmajer, to whom the poem is dedicated.

—Kazimierz Przerwa Tetmajer (1865-1940). Poet and novelist of the Young Poland period; a 'Ludźmierzak' by birth. His collection of stories *Na skalnym Podhalu* [In the Rocky Podhale region, 1903-1910] and his *Legenda Tatr* [Legend of the Tatras, 1912] played a role in popularising the culture of the mountainous Tatra regions among Poles.
—Autumn Night in Batignolles [Noc jesienna na Batignolles]. Published in *Ateneum*, 1938.
—Ballad of the Organgrinder [Ballada o kataryniarzu]. Published in *Czas*, 1939.

WORKS CITED

Primary sources

CZYŻEWSKI, Tytus. *Wiersze i utwory teatralne*, ed. Janusz Kryszak, Andrzej K. Waśkiewicz. Gdańsk: słowo/obraz terytoria, 2009.

CZYŻEWSKI, Tytus. *Zielone oko. Poezje formistyczne. Elektryczne wizje.* Kraków: Gebethner i spółka, 1920.

Secondary sources

APOLLINAIRE, Guillaume. *Alcools*. Paris: Gallimard, 2018.

APOLLINAIRE, Guillaume. *Calligrammes*. Paris: Gallimard, 2018.

BALUCH, Alicja. Baluch, 'Wizualność poezji Tytusa Czyżewskiego,' in *Rocznik naukowo-dydaktyczny* 101 (1986): 199-137.

CAMPBELL, Joseph. *Primitive Mythology*. London: Penguin, 1985.

DOBROWOLSKI, Tadeusz. *Malarstwo polskie ostatnich dwustu lat.* Wrocław: Ossolineum, 1989.

ELIADE, Mircea. *A History of Religious Ideas. Vol. 3: From Muhammed to the Age of Reforms.* Chicago: University of Chicago Press, 1988.

HORACE, *Carmina*. ed. P. Hofman Peerlkamp. Haarlem: Apud Vincentium Loosjes, 1834.

KONSTAŃCZAK, Stefan 'Od Formizmu do Strefizmu. Ewolucja poglądów estetycznych Leona Chwistka,' in *Słupskie studia filozoficzne*,8 (2009): 13-29.

KUNIŃSKA, Izabela, ed. *Sztuka świata. Leksykon A-K*. Warsaw: Arkady, 1998.

MIŁOSZ, Czesław. *The History of Polish Literature*. Berkeley: University of California Press, 400-401.

MORAWIŃSKA, Agnieszka. *Polish Painting, 15th to 20th Century.* Warszawa: Auriga, 1984.

OKOŃ, Jan. *Staopolskie pastorałki dramatyczne. Antologia.* Wrocław: Ossolineum, 1989.

ORDYŃSKA, Zofia. *To już prawie sto lat: pamiętnik aktorki.* Wrocław: Ossolineum, 1970.

PIOTROWSKI, Piotr. 'Od nacjonalizacji do socjalizacji polskiego modernizmu, 1913–1950,' in *Artium quaestiones* 15 (2004): 97-138.

PLEŚNIAROWICZ, Krzysztof. *Kantor.* Wrocław: Wydawnictwo Dolnośląskie, 1997.

PŁOSZEWSKI, Leon. *Wyspiański w oczach współczesnych.* Kraków: Wydawnictwo literackie, 1971.

POUND, Ezra. *ABC of Reading.* New York: New Directions, 1960.

SCHMIDT, Joël. *Słownik mitologii greckiej i rzymskiej.* Katowice: Wydawnictwo "Książnica", 1992.

STEINER, George. *After Babel. Aspects of Language and Translation.* Oxford: Oxford University Press, 1981.

STERN, Anatol. *Dom Apollinaire'a.* (Kraków: Wydawnictwo Literackie, 1973).

WAŁEK, Janusz. *Świat Wyspiańskiego.* Warsaw: Oficyna Wydawnicza "Nasza", 1994.

WAT, Aleksander. *Mój wiek.* Vol. I. Warsaw: Czytelnik, 1991.

ABOUT THE AUTHOR

Tytus Czyżewski (1880–1945) was a multifaceted artistic talent, creative in drama, poetry, and painting. His sometimes belligerent critical manifestos — included in this translation — helped establish the foundations of contemporary art in the early decades of the twentieth century. As a painter (he studied for a while under the tutelage of another great Polish polymath, the painter and poet Stanisław Wyspiański), he was associated with Expressionism and Formism (of which he was the main motor, in both painting and poetry). After his studies at the Academy of Fine Arts in Kraków, he spent some five years in Paris, where he came under the influence Picasso, the Cubists, and Cézanne in painting, and Guillaume Apollinaire in poetry. His poetry and plays, all of which are contained in this volume, are refreshingly disengaged, politically and patriotically, which marks him as fresh voice in the literary tradition of his homeland, and arguably makes his stunningly creative output more accessible to readers beyond Poland's borders. Chiefly concerned with form, he strove towards the 'anarchisation' and autonomy of the word and the poetic phrase, admittedly following in the footsteps of Apollinaire and Marinetti, both of whom he held in high esteem. Both his literary works and his painting are imbued with a radical modernism, which yet acknowledges the folk traditions of southern Poland, where he was born and spent most of his life. In this respect, and others, Czyżewski had a significant impact on the future of Polish art, in particular, that of another giant of contemporary painting and theatre, Tadeusz Kantor.

ABOUT THE TRANSLATOR

Charles S. Kraszewski (b. 1962) is a poet and translator. He is the author of three volumes of original verse (*Diet of Nails; Beast; Chanameed*). Several of his translations of Polish and Czech literature have been published by Glagoslav, among which may be found: Adam Mickiewicz's *Forefathers' Eve* (2016) and *Sonnets* (2018), Zygmunt Krasiński's *Dramatic Works* (2018), four plays of Juliusz Słowacki (2018), Stanisław Wyspiański's *Acropolis: the Wawel Plays* (2017) and the mock epics of Ignacy Kasicki (2019). His translations of the poetry of T.S. Eliot, Robinson Jeffers, and Lawrence Ferlinghetti into Polish have appeared in the Wrocław monthly *Odra*. Recently, his English version of Jan Kochanowski's *Dismissal of the Grecian Envoys* was produced at Shakespeare's Globe Theatre in London, under the direction of James Wallace. He is a member of the Union of Polish Writers Abroad (London) and of the Association of Polish Writers (SPP, Kraków).

Acropolis – The Wawel Plays
by Stanisław Wyspiański

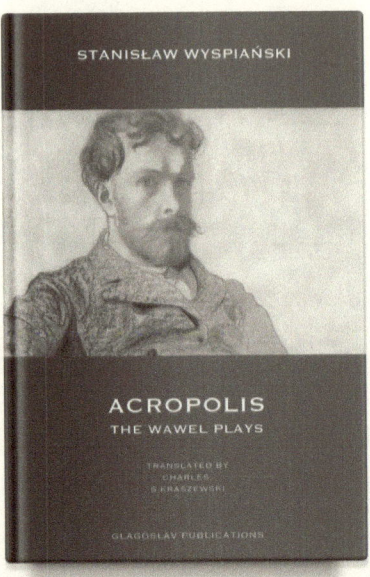

Stanisław Wyspiański (1869-1907) achieved worldwide fame, both as a painter, and Poland's greatest dramatist of the first half of the twentieth century. *Acropolis: the Wawel Plays*, brings together four of Wyspiański's most important dramatic works in a new English translation by Charles S. Kraszewski. All of the plays centre on Wawel Hill: the legendary seat of royal and ecclesiastical power in the poet's native city, the ancient capital of Poland. In these plays, Wyspiański explores the foundational myths of his nation: that of the self-sacrificial Wanda, and the struggle between King Bolesław the Bold and Bishop Stanisław Szczepanowski. In the eponymous play which brings the cycle to an end, Wyspiański carefully considers the value of myth to a nation without political autonomy, soaring in thought into an apocalyptic vision of the future. Richly illustrated with the poet's artwork, *Acropolis: the Wawel Plays* also contains Wyspiański's architectural proposal for the renovation of Wawel Hill, and a detailed critical introduction by the translator. In its plaited presentation of *Bolesław the Bold* and *Skałka*, the translation offers, for the first time, the two plays in the unified, composite format that the poet intended, but was prevented from carrying out by his untimely death.

Buy it > www.glagoslav.com

FOREFATHERS' EVE
by Adam Mickiewicz

Forefathers' Eve [*Dziady*] is a four-part dramatic work begun circa 1820 and completed in 1832 – with Part I published only after the poet's death, in 1860. The drama's title refers to *Dziady*, an ancient Slavic and Lithuanian feast commemorating the dead. This is the grand work of Polish literature, and it is one that elevates Mickiewicz to a position among the "great Europeans" such as Dante and Goethe.

With its Christian background of the Communion of the Saints, revenant spirits, and the interpenetration of the worlds of time and eternity, *Forefathers' Eve* speaks to men and women of all times and places. While it is a truly Polish work – Polish actors covet the role of Gustaw/Konrad in the same way that Anglophone actors covet that of Hamlet – it is one of the most universal works of literature written during the nineteenth century. It has been compared to Goethe's Faust – and rightfully so...

Buy it > www.glagoslav.com

Glagoslav Publications Catalogue

- *The Time of Women* by Elena Chizhova
- *Andrei Tarkovsky: A Life on the Cross* by Lyudmila Boyadzhieva
- *Sin* by Zakhar Prilepin
- *Hardly Ever Otherwise* by Maria Matios
- *Khatyn* by Ales Adamovich
- *The Lost Button* by Irene Rozdobudko
- *Christened with Crosses* by Eduard Kochergin
- *The Vital Needs of the Dead* by Igor Sakhnovsky
- *The Sarabande of Sara's Band* by Larysa Denysenko
- *A Poet and Bin Laden* by Hamid Ismailov
- *Zo Gaat Dat in Rusland* (Dutch Edition) by Maria Konjoekova
- *Kobzar* by Taras Shevchenko
- *The Stone Bridge* by Alexander Terekhov
- *Moryak* by Lee Mandel
- *King Stakh's Wild Hunt* by Uladzimir Karatkevich
- *The Hawks of Peace* by Dmitry Rogozin
- *Harlequin's Costume* by Leonid Yuzefovich
- *Depeche Mode* by Serhii Zhadan
- *Groot Slem en Andere Verhalen* (Dutch Edition) by Leonid Andrejev
- *METRO 2033* (Dutch Edition) by Dmitry Glukhovsky
- *METRO 2034* (Dutch Edition) by Dmitry Glukhovsky
- *A Russian Story* by Eugenia Kononenko
- *Herstories, An Anthology of New Ukrainian Women Prose Writers*
- *The Battle of the Sexes Russian Style* by Nadezhda Ptushkina
- *A Book Without Photographs* by Sergey Shargunov
- *Down Among The Fishes* by Natalka Babina
- *disUNITY* by Anatoly Kudryavitsky
- *Sankya* by Zakhar Prilepin
- *Wolf Messing* by Tatiana Lungin
- *Good Stalin* by Victor Erofeyev
- *Solar Plexus* by Rustam Ibragimbekov
- *Don't Call me a Victim!* by Dina Yafasova
- *Poetin* (Dutch Edition) by Chris Hutchins and Alexander Korobko

- *A History of Belarus* by Lubov Bazan
- *Children's Fashion of the Russian Empire* by Alexander Vasiliev
- *Empire of Corruption: The Russian National Pastime* by Vladimir Soloviev
- *Heroes of the 90s: People and Money. The Modern History of Russian Capitalism* by Alexander Solovev, Vladislav Dorofeev and Valeria Bashkirova
- *Fifty Highlights from the Russian Literature* (Dutch Edition) by Maarten Tengbergen
- *Bajesvolk* (Dutch Edition) by Michail Chodorkovsky
- *Dagboek van Keizerin Alexandra* (Dutch Edition)
- *Myths about Russia* by Vladimir Medinskiy
- *Boris Yeltsin: The Decade that Shook the World* by Boris Minaev
- *A Man Of Change: A study of the political life of Boris Yeltsin*
- *Sberbank: The Rebirth of Russia's Financial Giant* by Evgeny Karasyuk
- *To Get Ukraine* by Oleksandr Shyshko
- *Asystole* by Oleg Pavlov
- *Gnedich* by Maria Rybakova
- *Marina Tsvetaeva: The Essential Poetry*
- *Multiple Personalities* by Tatyana Shcherbina
- *The Investigator* by Margarita Khemlin
- *The Exile* by Zinaida Tulub
- *Leo Tolstoy: Flight from Paradise* by Pavel Basinsky
- *Moscow in the 1930* by Natalia Gromova
- *Laurus* (Dutch edition) by Evgenij Vodolazkin
- *Prisoner* by Anna Nemzer
- *The Crime of Chernobyl: The Nuclear Goulag* by Wladimir Tchertkoff
- *Alpine Ballad* by Vasil Bykau
- *The Complete Correspondence of Hryhory Skovoroda*
- *The Tale of Aypi* by Ak Welsapar
- *Selected Poems* by Lydia Grigorieva
- *The Fantastic Worlds of Yuri Vynnychuk*
- *The Garden of Divine Songs and Collected Poetry of Hryhory Skovoroda*
- *Adventures in the Slavic Kitchen: A Book of Essays with Recipes* by Igor Klekh
- *Seven Signs of the Lion* by Michael M. Naydan

- *Forefathers' Eve* by Adam Mickiewicz
- *One-Two* by Igor Eliseev
- *Girls, be Good* by Bojan Babić
- *Time of the Octopus* by Anatoly Kucherena
- *The Grand Harmony* by Bohdan Ihor Antonych
- *The Selected Lyric Poetry Of Maksym Rylsky*
- *The Shining Light* by Galymkair Mutanov
- *The Frontier: 28 Contemporary Ukrainian Poets - An Anthology*
- *Acropolis: The Wawel Plays* by Stanisław Wyspiański
- *Contours of the City* by Attyla Mohylny
- *Conversations Before Silence: The Selected Poetry of Oles Ilchenko*
- *The Secret History of my Sojourn in Russia* by Jaroslav Hašek
- *Mirror Sand: An Anthology of Russian Short Poems*
- *Maybe We're Leaving* by Jan Balaban
- *Death of the Snake Catcher* by Ak Welsapar
- *A Brown Man in Russia* by Vijay Menon
- *Hard Times* by Ostap Vyshnia
- *The Flying Dutchman* by Anatoly Kudryavitsky
- *Nikolai Gumilev's Africa* by Nikolai Gumilev
- *Combustions* by Srđan Srdić
- *The Sonnets* by Adam Mickiewicz
- *Dramatic Works* by Zygmunt Krasiński
- *Four Plays* by Juliusz Słowacki
- *Little Zinnobers* by Elena Chizhova
- *We Are Building Capitalism! Moscow in Transition 1992-1997* by Robert Stephenson
- *The Nuremberg Trials* by Alexander Zvyagintsev
- *The Hemingway Game* by Evgeni Grishkovets
- *A Flame Out at Sea* by Dmitry Novikov
- *Jesus' Cat* by Grig
- *Want a Baby and Other Plays* by Sergei Tretyakov
- *Mikhail Bulgakov: The Life and Times* by Marietta Chudakova
- *Leonardo's Handwriting* by Dina Rubina
- *A Burglar of the Better Sort* by Tytus Czyżewski
- *The Mouseiad and other Mock Epics* by Ignacy Krasicki
- *Ravens before Noah* by Susanna Harutyunyan

- *An English Queen and Stalingrad* by Natalia Kulishenko
- *Point Zero* by Narek Malian
- *Absolute Zero* by Artem Chekh
- *Olanda* by Rafał Wojasiński
- *Robinsons* by Aram Pachyan
- *The Monastery* by Zakhar Prilepin
- *The Selected Poetry of Bohdan Rubchak: Songs of Love, Songs of Death, Songs of the Moon*
- *Mebet* by Alexander Grigorenko
- *The Orchestra* by Vladimir Gonik
- *Everyday Stories* by Mima Mihajlović
- *Slavdom* by Ľudovít Štúr
- *The Code of Civilization* by Vyacheslav Nikonov
- *Where Was the Angel Going?* by Jan Balaban
- *De Zwarte Kip* (Dutch Edition) by Antoni Pogorelski
- *Głosy / Voices* by Jan Polkowski
- *Sergei Tretyakov: A Revolutionary Writer in Stalin's Russia* by Robert Leach
- *Opstand* (Dutch Edition) by Władysław Reymont
- *Dramatic Works* by Cyprian Kamil Norwid
- *Children's First Book of Chess* by Natalie Shevando and Matthew McMillion
- *Precursor* by Vasyl Shevchuk
- *The Vow: A Requiem for the Fifties* by Jiří Kratochvil
- *De Bibliothecaris* (Dutch edition) by Mikhail Jelizarov
- *Subterranean Fire* by Natalka Bilotserkivets
- *Vladimir Vysotsky: Selected Works*
- *Behind the Silk Curtain* by Gulistan Khamzayeva
- *The Village Teacher and Other Stories* by Theodore Odrach
- *Duel* by Borys Antonenko-Davydovych
- *War Poems* by Alexander Korotko
- *Ballads and Romances* by Adam Mickiewicz
- *The Revolt of the Animals* by Wladyslaw Reymont
- *Poems about my Psychiatrist* by Andrzej Kotański
- *Someone Else's Life* by Elena Dolgopyat
- *Liza's Waterfall: The hidden story of a Russian feminist* by Pavel Basinsky
- *Biography of Sergei Prokofiev* by Igor Vishnevetsky

More coming...

GLAGOSLAV PUBLICATIONS
www.glagoslav.com

www.ingramcontent.com/pod-product-compliance
Lightning Source LLC
Chambersburg PA
CBHW031057080526
44587CB00011B/726